Think You Can't Sing?
Think Again!

This book is for you if...

- You were asked to mime when singing in school

- You were rejected from the school choir

- People tell you you can't sing

- Your parents told you that you're tone-deaf

- You believe you can't sing

- People laugh at you when you sing

- People tell you that you sing out-of-tune

- You'd love to join a choir but you think you're not good enough

- You believe you might be tone-deaf, but haven't had this confirmed

- Your confidence in your voice has been undermined

- You're scared to sing in public

- You think you have a terrible voice

- You're confident enough to sing karaoke but everyone always laughs

- You have a friend or relative who can identify with one or more of the above statements

Resources

Sales page for the book

Here's where you can see a summary of what the book is about, purchase additional copies of the book, and where you can send your friends when you're recommending the book to them: **www.thinkyoucantsing.com**

Resource page for those who have purchased the book

I'd appreciate it if you didn't share this with others, as it's only supposed to be for people who have actually bought the book. Go to this page for more resources, including the accompanying videos for this book, up-to-date news and links to the various communities in which you can participate: **www.tycsta.com**

If you're looking for a singing family to join, have a look at London City Voices, London's friendliest choir:
www.londoncityvoices.co.uk

Richard Swan

Richard Swan was born in South Africa, schooled in Ireland and studied music at Goldsmiths, University of London. He has worked as a choir-director, educator, author, bandleader and composer ever since. He has had music commissioned by Hampton Court Palace and has collaborated with Annie Lennox. He is the founder of London City Voices, a huge non-audition pop choir in London, and composes in styles ranging from film music to drum 'n' bass. He has directed choirs at the Royal Albert Hall, Wembley Stadium, Hackney Empire and Troxy. His passion is making music accessible for everyone, and he regularly runs workshops to get people singing together in harmony, regardless of previous experience. He runs piano singalongs at festivals around the UK and at venues in London, and has a repertoire of hundreds of songs.

Design and illustration by Rachael Dunstan

Cover design and illustration by Richard Swan and Rachael Dunstan

For more information about the author and further materials,
visit www.londoncityvoices.co.uk.

ISBN details

978-1-7394724-0-5 (Paperback)

978-1-7394724-1-2 (e-book)

978-1-7394724-2-9 (Audiobook)

978-1-7394724-3-6 (Hardback)

Typeset in 10pt Cera and Rachaelscribes

To my parents, Eric & Joan Swan.
I wish you could have seen this.
Thank you for the passion for
music which you instilled in me.

What people are saying

Joyous and kind, a singing handbook like no other

This is a wonderful book for anyone who has ever been put off singing

Warm and encouraging, reading this makes me feel like I can sing after all!

The "can't sing" myth banished for good

Give this book a go if you are even a little curious about your voice

To be gently guided away from fear and self-consciousness towards fun and freedom is a wonderful thing

This is like a conversation with your favourite teacher - insightful, challenging and encouraging

This book has helped me find my voice and changed my future

ACKNOWLEDGEMENTS

This book has been a labour of love for the last three years. I started it during the first COVID lockdown, and have been pretty obsessed with it since then, although it has not always been possible to work on it as much as I would have liked. I have since discovered a passion for writing, about which I'm tremendously delighted and excited. It's important to note, however, that there is no way that I could have completed this project without the following beautiful people.

Firstly, my fantastic wife Kate, who has diligently edited vast portions of this book. Additionally she has kept encouraging me and has let me Swan off to Thanet to spend several weekends writing by the sea. Thank you for believing in me, for not getting too grumpy with me when I leave things everywhere, and for the support you give me daily. And for teaching me the difference between 'which' and 'that'. I love you.

My incredible illustrator, typesetter and designer, Rachael Dunstan, who has surpassed all expectations with her beautiful drawings. Rachael, I'm incredibly grateful to you for bringing my ideas to life in such succinct, humorous and often poignant ways. Also, your patience during the editing process has been limitless. Thank you SO much.

My marvellous sons, Matty and Ben Swan, both of them brilliant, talented musicians and lovely, kind men, who have listened to their dad drone on about his magnificent book for quite a long time now. Thank you both for your friendship, love, encouragement and support throughout. I love you both more than I can adequately express.

My coach, Jaqueline Norton, without whom this project would have just stayed an idea in my head. She helped me take this concept and develop it into something concrete. Most of all, she helped me to recognise areas of my life where I showed 'resistance', and to work on myself. Jacq, that's an ongoing process, but I'm very grateful for the tools you gave me with which I can continue to do this.

My very good friend Cliff Fluet, for introducing me to Jacqueline in the first place, for the professional advice, for always encouraging me along the way, for very wise words and lots of laughs and puns. I also know you like a double-entendre, so I'll give you one later.

I have discussed many of the concepts in this book with Dr Fiona Brand, particularly when she was studying for her PhD and we shared some accountability. Fi, never have I met someone as readily distracted from work as myself, or with the same shared passion for biscuits. I hope you recognise your influence on this book.

My dear friend Amy Kirkwood, who has an annoying knack for completely disa rming me and getting me to say exactly what's on my mind, and then getting me to work out how to solve it. Amy, you're a great friend and a genius coach. And, it turns out, a talented editor with a real eye for detail! Thank you always for your wise words, and the time you have put into helping with this project.

Catherine Allison – brilliant friend, sounding-board, colleague, encourager, I'm thankful for hilarious but productive conversations, lots of invented words, ferocious hangovers, SEO and you always being my cheerleader. Wharves.

My wonderful friend Mandy Stone has been a massive encouragement throughout the years that I've known her, and I would not be where I am today without her support, both practical and emotional. Thank you Mandy, for all of it. You're rather lovely.

Phil Mackenzie – my great friend, you're one of the few people I've successfully collaborated with on anything. I always enjoy our long rambling conversations about music, business, philosophy, marketing, gadgets, DIY and all the other stuff. You continue to be an inspiration. Thank you.

Jennifer Geary – for great advice on self-publishing. I'm incredibly thankful for your help with this – you demystified the process so well for me and I really value your experience.

David Hughes, my old BNI friend, thank you for introducing me to the arcane art of advertising and marketing, and particularly YouTube. I've always very much valued your advice, and it's stood me in good stead.

To Garry Lace and the Storians team. It's been a pleasure working with you to get this out in front of people. The world needs more harmony. Let's make it happen

To my amazing choir, London City Voices, for basically letting me earn a living by playing around and having fun, and for putting me in contact with most of the people who inspired and helped me to write this book.

Dr Ashok Jansari, for helping me to understand some of the science behind how memory works.

Dr Frank Russo from the University of Toronto, for spending time chatting to me about his experience with amusia.

To the seagulls of Thanet, whose voices will always bring me inspiration, laughter, peace and a sense of belonging. Oh, and a little bit of fear. I think you probably know more about me than anyone.

To all of my Beta Readers – thank you for taking the time to be honest about your thoughts. I appreciate it very much and I DON'T TAKE ANY OF IT PERSONALLY AT ALL. IT'S FINE!

And to my courageous guinea-pigs, who have been brave enough to take the plunge and trust me enough to risk embarrassing themselves. You are all fantastic.

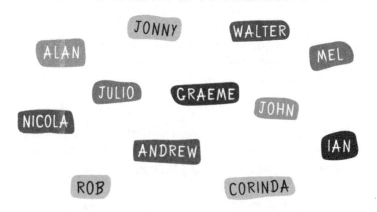

How to find the voice
you never thought you'd have

Richard Swan

with illustrations by Rachael Dunstan

CONTENTS

Introduction   21

01. Hard Evidence   35

02. Just the Basic Facts   38

03. Barriers to Singing   49

04. Control   60

05. Both Easier and Harder Than You Think   70

06. Aiming   80

07. The Honest Self-Critic   87

08. Being Fully Present and Aware   94

09. The Phenomenon of 'Happy Birthday'   105

10. Some Useful Theory   116

11. A Bit of Biology   124

12. Memory, Muscle Memory and Waypoints   132

13. Making Footprints   142

14. Lost in the Crowd   152

15. Success Stories   158

16. Wrapping It Up   172

Appendix: Congenital Amusia   181

INTRODUCTION

During my working life, I've been struck by how many people I come into contact with who are convinced that they are completely unable to sing, despite the fact that congenital amusia – the scientific name for the musical equivalent of colourblindness – affects such a very small percentage of people.*

If you believe that you cannot sing, the fact is that you are most likely to be wrong. Perhaps you cannot sing *yet*. Most people who think that they can't sing do have the capability of doing so – there are just a few hurdles getting in the way.

Without doubt, the biggest one of these hurdles is your mindset. You don't believe you can do it. I want to change this. I meet people on a weekly basis who all their lives have laboured under the misapprehension that they cannot sing, and I can usually deal with that issue in a few short sessions with them.

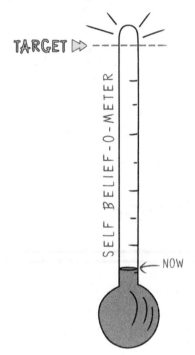

Some people take a bit more work, and a very small percentage may never totally get the hang of it. This, however, is often down to a lack of self-confidence and thus a lack of commitment to seeing the project through, as they don't really believe it can be done. It's often less about your ability than about your willingness to be vulnerable, to accept that your opinion about your own voice may be wrong, and your desire to change that. Believe me, I do understand that there is some security in that assurance that says 'I'm a rubbish singer', and you can hide safely there. If you insist hard enough that you're a terrible singer, people won't ask you to do it, so you can avoid the embarrassment and the exposure. However, I'm here to challenge that. I have written this book with the express purpose of drawing you out of that hiding place, and making you really think about this whole thing a bit more. You're reading the book, so you're at least acknowledging that you have an interest in finding out more. I'll give you a heads-up though. You're going to have to take some risks. If you don't, you'll never make any progress.

NEEDED

☑ WILLINGNESS TO BE VULNERABLE

☑ TRUST IN AN EXPERT

☐ BELIEF I CAN SING!

And so... welcome! I'm genuinely delighted that you're here. If you believe that you can't sing, this book is specifically and carefully designed for YOU. You are not an afterthought – you are the sole focus of this book.

I have done lots of research to find out what was out there for people who think that they can't sing, and the result was: precious little. There are a lot of YouTube lessons, many of dubious quality, which are stuck on the end of someone's vocal coaching channel because they thought that it would be a good idea to capture a bit of that market. There are a couple of online paid-for courses, which I subscribed to myself and watched. To be absolutely honest, I spent most of that time with my head in my hands, shouting questions at the screen: 'Why would you bring this information here? It's irrelevant!' and 'Nobody wants to sing that song, it's a children's song from the 1940s!'

This book is not like that.

This book is written predominantly to help you overcome the biggest obstacle that stands between yourself and a life that involves some singing. This obstacle is your mindset. There is a limit to the amount of practical work we can do in a book, because singing is a physical activity. No amount of the written word will allow me to actually show you personally how to sing, in the same way that, for example, if I were teaching you to dive, or play football, or defend yourself on the street, at some point there would need to be some physical demonstration.

Thanks to technology, I have provided some exercises and demonstrations on the accompanying website, which will definitely help you on the practical side. These are not totally interactive (ie, I can't tell if you're getting them right or not) but they should be very useful, and should be considered an essential part of the book.

There are various YouTube examples from other people peppered throughout the book. Hopefully these will remain live in the future, but the links and QR codes are hosted on my own site, and therefore editable after publication. If you should come across a broken link, please email contact@thinkyoucantsing.com to let us know, and we'll redirect it to a working link as soon as we can.

How to read this book

Firstly, navigate to **www.TYCSTA.com** and bookmark it. This is your resources page, and you'll need to have this available. It's not linked from any other websites, and it's not searchable on Google, so if you think you'll forget the link, it's best to bookmark.

Ideally, you'll read the book and watch the videos when you're told to do so. However, I realise that not everyone does this sort of thing (I certainly don't!). You will learn a lot from the book without the videos. You will learn a lot from the videos without the book. If you do indulge in both, you'll probably find it easier to leave your video-watching device on the resources page and simply navigate to the next video when needed, rather than constantly using the links and/or QR codes. I've put those in there so that you've always got a way of getting to the right video, but it might be a little bit fiddly if you keep having to jump back and forwards.

I've also put a TLDR (Too Long, Didn't Read) list in at the end of lots of the chapters. This is really meant to consolidate your learning by summarising the key take-away points from the chapter.

Go and watch the video introduction at this link:

 https://lcv.pub/tycstaintro

These videos are not behind any sort of paywall, so they're available for the world to watch. However, they make the most sense in the context of the book that you are currently reading. There is lots in the book that is not covered in the videos.

Firstly, however, the most important work needs to be done in your head. This is the beginning of your journey. I hope it will be a life-changing experience. That's not hyperbole by the way. I've seen people's entire lives turned around by suddenly discovering, often later in life, that they had a voice. It's given them new confidence, and from that, new friendships, relationships and even new jobs. In fact, there have even been a couple of babies born as a result of people joining my choir.

I firmly believe that this book will give you something of tremendous value. It will hopefully move you into a different headspace, and lead you to a different relationship with your voice than the one you currently have. For most of you this negative mindset really is the biggest hurdle to overcome. My dream is that this book will be the tool that will unlock the voices of millions of people around the world. I'd recommend you finish this book before you embark on any singing course, singing lessons or personal coaching, as that will ensure that you've understood my philosophy and my take on how it all works. It will also prepare you for any setbacks in the future which might demoralise you, such as engaging the wrong singing teacher (this can have a devastating effect).

My mission

My goal with this book is, first and foremost, to change lives. It is to open up to you the world of participatory music, especially singing. Like any creator, I will be overjoyed if my product becomes successful, but I am creating these products because I believe that I am very good at teaching this stuff, and the things that I teach and the method I use seem to make people happy. I want all those shots of serotonin when people email me (and please do!) to say how much they're enjoying singing in a choir, or performing at open mic events, or just being able to sing 'Happy Birthday' to their children without feeling embarrassed.

My background

I've worked in various roles as a musician over the last 30 years. I've been a choir director, a composer, an arranger, a bandleader and an educator. I've taught in secondary schools and I've been fortunate enough to conduct at the Royal Albert Hall. But all the way through this journey, I remain a teacher by vocation. Teaching is the thing I do pretty much all the time, whether that's part of my job description or not. I love seeing the penny drop when a previously hidden fact or skill or seemingly arcane piece of knowledge suddenly reveals itself to a student or client, and I absolutely adore watching someone making progress in an activity. Over the years, my passion has been to make music more accessible for people who aren't particularly musically educated. I trained and worked as a secondary school music teacher in London for many years, and my main thrust was always getting the children to participate, whatever their ability or experience. I ran bands, orchestras and choirs, and introduced music technology into the classrooms. I always made a point of hiring fun, dynamic instrumental teachers, and together we turned music departments into vibrant, exciting places to be, where lots of the 'naughty kids' would come and spend their lunchtimes working on their music projects.

I remember an occasion in one school when the deputy headteacher walked into my classroom one lunchtime to find about 15 of the stroppiest year 11s (16-year olds) totally engaged in their various music technology productions, raising their hands to politely ask for my help when they needed it. He was blown away, as he'd written off many of these students as lazy, unmotivated and troublesome. I rarely had any problem with any of them, as they loved my subject.

For years I have been involved in running events, and in 2009 I started a monthly Live Band Karaoke session at the Hootananny in Brixton in South London, which ran for 11 years before COVID finally put paid to it. This has always been about enabling untrained people to get involved with music, and giving people that 'rockstar' experience.
In 2012 I started London City Voices, a non-audition pop choir in the City of London. When we started, we had between six and 12 people for most of the first year. 11 years later there are approximately 550 active members across several nights a week, and we've seen over 3000 people come through the doors over the past decade. Lockdown wasn't great for us, and it decimated our numbers, but we've built back up again and we usually have several new people attending every night each week.

 https://lcv.pub/TYCSTALCV

My expertise

I want to make another point here. I really do know what I'm talking about. I really mean that. I've spent years teaching people to find their voices. I have come across just about every type of barrier to singing that there is, and I have succeeded in teaching 100% of the people that I've worked with to pitch correctly. You'll probably think that you have a dreadful voice, but please understand this. Your voice itself isn't particularly bad. No one's is. Do people put their hands over their ears when you speak? No. Well then. Some people just haven't learned to sing well, or at all. Most of the time this can be corrected. Don't be a diva and flounce about saying, 'Oh I'm the most terrible singer, you can't do anything with my voice.' I probably can, and you need to get used to this, or else there's no point in reading any further. So, if you still have this attitude, please read this last paragraph again. You may have loads of negative beliefs about your singing voice because of things people have said to you in the past – we'll cover some of those shortly. I want you to replace those negative thoughts with the following statement.

— **The people in my life who have been critical about my voice were not qualified to judge. Richard Swan, an expert in teaching people to sing, believes that my voice has potential. I choose to believe him.**

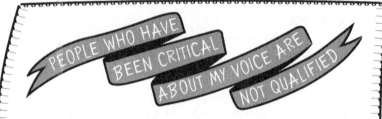

BY READING THIS BOOK, I

UNDERSTAND THAT

= MY VOICE HAS =

POTENTIAL

BELIEVED BY

ℓS

RICHARD SWAN

WHO HAS LOTS OF EXPERIENCE
IN ENCOURAGING PEOPLE TO SING

What I'm saying is, I don't want you to put your trust in yourself at this stage, as that has already been undermined. Instead, I want you to put your trust in me. I know what I'm talking about. Your voice is not terrible. Your pitching might be inaccurate, but that can be worked on. Let's do this.

Too Long, Didn't Read (TLDR)

- This book is written for you, and people like you.

- Your biggest obstacle to being a better singer is your own (lack of) self-belief.

- I'm extremely well qualified to help you.

- I'm passionate about helping people like you.

- You're very unlikely to be actually tone-deaf.

- Trust me.

Now move on to the next chapter, **Hard Evidence**.

* If you actually think you might have congenital amusia, see the appendix at the end of the book. You can even do an online test to find out if you do. However, it's very unlikely. Going forward, I am going to make claims about what I can teach you to do. My single all-encompassing caveat here is that we'll assume you don't have amusia, as most people do not.

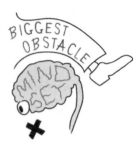

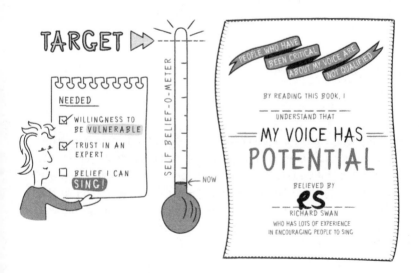

HARD EVIDENCE

When we embark on any learning journey, it's important that we're able to measure progress. To do this, we need a benchmark so we can see where we started. So, I need you to do something for me.

Head over to the website, watch this video, and do what it says:

https://lcv.pub/TYCSTA01

If you're not able to watch at this moment, it's a video asking you to record yourself singing a song that you know, warts and all. Do it as well as you can at this stage. Don't worry about it sounding awful. In some ways, if this all goes the way I expect it to, the worse it is, the better the outcome in the long term. You're going to feel some resistance to this task, and you'll probably try to find reasons not to do it, but I **really** want you to do it.

In fact, I'll go as far as to say that if you don't do it, you won't have completed the tasks properly, and you'll be sabotaging your own efforts. It's really important to document the stage you are at now, so the more you can capture of your current level of singing, the more you'll be able to look back and say, 'This is how far I've come.'

This has a lot to do with trusting me. Right now you see little point in doing this as you probably don't believe you'll get any better. But I know more than you do about this. I know that it's very likely that you're going to improve beyond anything you thought possible, and you're then going to wish that you had some evidence to show what you were like before.

So please, humour me. Make the recording, or even better, the recordings, now. Do a couple of songs if you want. It doesn't have to be amazing quality, it can be on your phone. Ideally, do it with a backing track, but that's not essential. What is essential is that you capture yourself singing before you've had any lessons from me.

When you've done this, move on to the next chapter, **Just the Basic Facts**.

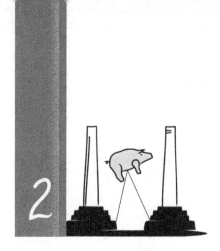

JUST THE BASIC FACTS

Before I give you some facts about singing, let's start with a little video about tuning:

https://lcv.pub/TYCSTA02

Ok, now you've watched the video, hopefully you understand how tuning works. This is a basic truth that you need to understand, but it's one of those things that people don't often explain, as they think that everyone instinctively understands it.

Normalising the dissonance

One of the reasons why people often don't sing in tune when they're singing along with music is that they have normalised the dissonance. Let me explain.

Dissonance can be described as a lack of harmony among musical notes. It's when you hear notes clashing, and they don't sound very nice. Sometimes it can be deliberate. Many musicians make a feature out of dissonance, and in the same way that poems don't have to rhyme and art doesn't have to look like the object it is depicting, music doesn't have to sound 'nice' (which is a subjective term anyway). But in most popular genres of music, 'nice-sounding' is the order of the day. We don't expect songs to sound unpleasant to the ear. Going back to the tuning video above, when you hear the note just before it's in tune, it sounds dissonant and unpleasant. Or rather... it should.

What you may have done over the years is this: because no one has ever taken the time to correct your singing (they may have criticised it, but not actually shown you how to improve), you have acclimatised yourself to hearing the dissonance when you're out-of-tune. This is a bit like when people get used to a bitter taste or an unusual smell, and end up actually accepting it – indeed, perhaps even liking it. The result of this is that you no longer feel the need to correct yourself when you're off-key, as it's a sound that you're used to. You're going to have to retrain yourself to notice when there is a dissonance happening, so that this triggers you to then find the correct note.

Voice range

We're all born with unique voices. Some are pitched low, some high, some in the middle. None of these are right or wrong, they just are, in the same way that some people are big, some are small and some are medium. There is no right type of voice. Our voices change throughout our lives. Testosterone has a massive effect on voices, so you generally get that huge change in sound for boys when they hit puberty and their voices deepen. We all have a **range** – this means our highest and lowest notes, and all of the notes in between – and with practice this can be significantly extended. Even with training, however, we all have a preferred range, and this will define what **voice** we are. Traditionally, and simplistically, I'll label these as **soprano** (high female), **alto** (low female), **tenor** (high male) and **bass** (low male). Note that these are for adult voices. These aren't exclusive, and the gender allocation is in no way determined, but almost all sopranos and altos will be female. My choir actually has several female tenors and even a female bass. Trans and non-binary people will find that they vary massively on this, so it's harder to categorise on a general level. For what it's worth, I'm a bass. I can sing higher than many tenors can, but the difference is that I can't sustain it for long. I can demonstrate really high notes to the tenors (and altos, and sopranos) in my choir, but if I have to sing up in their range for an entire song, it will exhaust me and I'll start to become hoarse.

I go into a bit more detail about this in the chapter **A Bit of Biology**.

The 'experience gap'

I've come to realise that there is a big void of knowledge, or 'experience gap', in the heads of people who have NOT grown up being able to sing. There is a combination of myths that they believe and facts that they are unaware of, which seem obvious to those of us who have always sung.

I'll take the opportunity at this point to distinguish between two different things that people mean when they say they can't sing. Some people are talking about their **tone** and others are referring to their **pitch**.

Tone (and accent)

Some people say that they can't sing because they think that the quality of their voice isn't great. It might be scratchy, husky, weak, hoarse or thin. It might even be to do with accent, and not having learned to make the mouth shapes that will let them sing in an accepted style.

These are things that can generally be easily improved with a vocal coach, who can teach you about the physicality of how you actually produce the sounds. I'm not going to focus massively on tone in this book, as that's something that you can work on later with a singing teacher. Most singing teachers will happily teach someone who hasn't got a great tone, but lots of them will refuse to work with people who can't pitch.

One point I will make, though, is that if you want to sound like a particular artist – say, Amy Winehouse, or Frank Sinatra for example – you're going to have to attempt to mimic how they pronounce words while they sing. You really have to try to imitate them. Maybe you have a Cockney accent when you speak normally, but you want to sound like Dean Martin singing 'Sway'. If so, you'll have to put on an American accent when you sing. If you want to sound like Lily Allen but you have quite a posh English accent, you'll have to do some work on your impersonation first, as this will impact how you sound. It's usually to do with how you say and sing vowel sounds, and whether or not you use diphthongs (when a word has two different vowel sounds next to each other, like the word 'boy', which is made up of two vowel sounds – 'aww' and 'ee'). Many people find this level of impersonating quite embarrassing, so they never really commit to it, and hence never manage to sound like they want to. As I say, this isn't really what we're dealing with in this book, as it's not what most people mean when they say they can't sing. Hopefully though, the above points may help you if that's something you struggle with.

Pitch

Most people who say they can't sing actually mean that they can't hold a tune. They find it hard to match the pitches of the song that they're trying to sing. This can manifest in different ways and at different levels of severity. Perhaps you know that you're not tone-deaf (ie, you can recognise a tune, notice when you're not singing the right notes, etc) but you just can't seem to hit the correct notes most of the time. Perhaps you really believe that you're tone-deaf, and you have no idea about any of it.

You might sing on a bit of a monotone, probably on a note that bears no relation to any of the notes that are supposed to be sung. You might sing some bits perfectly, but then when there's a high note you don't get anywhere near it. That last one is the easiest to deal with, and if you identify with that, you'll definitely be able to learn to get those notes.

One thing you should realise is that not all singing teachers are good at helping people who struggle with pitching.

Many people, including some singing teachers, believe that there are lots of people who simply don't possess the ability to sing. I believe that they're wrong, but there is a huge culture that says, erroneously, that this is true. Not everyone understands what I'm telling you here. In

45

fact, most people think the opposite, and many singing teachers don't realise that you can be trained to pitch accurately.

Some of them do realise it, but they only want to teach 'proper singers' (ie, people who can already sing well but would like to get better at it). The latter is fine – we all make our career choices – but I want to make the point that **just because you saw a singing teacher and they said you were tone-deaf doesn't mean that you are.**

Right, let's recap:

TLDR

- We all have different voices, some high, some low.

- Some of you believe things about singing, and about singers, that aren't true at all.

- Some of you are unaware of some basic facts about singing and singers.

- Some people, when they say they can't sing, are referring to their tone, which is relatively easy to change.

- Most people, when they say they can't sing, mean that they can't hit the right notes. This requires a bit of knowledge and a bit of work.

— Just because a singing teacher said that you can't sing, doesn't mean that it's true. Trust me.

In the next chapter, we're going to look at some of these barriers that stop people singing. However, before we do that, head over to the website to do some pitching practice. But first, I'll just explain something. For some of the exercises, I've created two versions of the video – one for low voices and one for high voices. I've touched on this briefly at the beginning of this chapter, but for most people, **low voices = men** and **high voices = women**. However, this may not always be the case, so if you're struggling in one, try the other.

Off you go. When you've finished, go on to the next chapter, **Barriers to Singing**.

LOW VOICES

https://lcv.pub/TYCSTA03low

HIGH VOICES

https://lcv.pub/TYCSTA03high

BARRIERS TO SINGING

There are many things that stop people singing well, but it all boils down to five areas. Let's take a look at those now.

1. Lack of confidence

As I've already mentioned, this can be a huge issue for people. Some people had a parent who decided that their own lack of tunefulness was in some way inherited from one of their parents, and determined that this would carry on down the generations. Despite having zero credentials about how pitch and singing work, they confidently bestow their wisdom on the child: 'Your granny couldn't carry a tune in her head, neither can I, and neither can you! Tone-deaf, the lot of us!' Or some such nonsense.

Other people have their teachers to blame. You wouldn't believe how many adults I meet who tell me they were told to mime by their music teacher, or thrown out of the school choir. One recent pupil of mine said that he went to a Catholic school, and he remembers that when the Bishop was coming to visit the class, their nun teacher took him and four other boys aside and instructed them, 'Now, when we're singing the hymns, you five open your mouths but don't utter a sound!'

Other people have had their confidence destroyed by their friends and colleagues, whether as a child or an adult (or often, both). People can be cruel, and also incredibly quick to pick on someone who isn't conforming to the norm. I know this, as I was always rubbish at football at school, and my classmates made sure that I was aware of this at any opportunity.

These things, while they may seem to be a good opportunity for a little joke or self-deprecation later in life, actually cause us emotional pain, and can often lead to a lifetime of not being able to enjoy the incredible catharsis of singing. I find this unbelievably sad, and so I've made it something of a mission in my life to re-enable 'lost singers'. It's amazing how rooted this conviction can be. So many people argue with me because they have a deep-seated belief that they truly are tone-deaf, whereas in reality the basis for their belief is merely an off-the-cuff comment from an ill-informed teacher, friend, colleague or parent.

An aside about singing teachers
I want to make this very clear: a teacher who doesn't properly understand how to help a person who thinks they can't sing can be the biggest obstacle to someone discovering their voice. A person who is scared of their own voice will assume that the teacher is correct when they say authoritatively, 'You can't sing.' Understandably, they will assume that the singing teacher knows what they are talking about, and will therefore use them as evidence that they're incapable of learning to sing.

The (high) number of times that I have had to argue with someone because their singing teacher said they were tone-deaf makes me very sad indeed. Singing teachers and vocal coaches are there to whip the already-competent voice into better shape. They're not really trained to help people learn the skill of pitching. To use another analogy, if you want to learn to run more effectively, you might hire a personal trainer or sports coach to work with. However, if you've had an accident, you've been in a wheelchair, and you need to learn to walk again, you would be much better going to a physical therapist – someone who really knows how the brain and body learn together at the beginning of the process. It's a different discipline. I'm aware this analogy isn't quite right, as the person is learning to walk again, rather than for the first time, but I'm sure you get the idea. I'm not saying that singing teachers are bad – lots of them are amazing – but I'm saying that they don't always get it right, and this is a very misunderstood area.

2. Your expectations are too high

This is part of the 'experience gap' I mentioned in the last chapter. A really important piece of information to take in here is this: 'normal' people (ie, people who can sing just as much as anyone else, not X-Factor stars) get it wrong a LOT of the time, and they are perfectly aware of this. Lots of them sing flat, sharp and even completely incorrectly sometimes. This is quite normal.

After a lot of practice, normal people may be able to sing a piece of music pretty correctly all the way through, but still may fluff bits. This is why singing is an art and not a science. It's not like a maths problem, where there is a definitive answer. Even the most accomplished singer will have days where they're really not on their game, and they will get things wrong.

Most often, the only difference between a 'singer' and a 'non-singer' is simply their attitude to getting it wrong.

A singer will think 'Oops, I got that note wrong, but I'm generally ok at singing. I'll just make sure I look out for that bit next time.' A non-singer will take every note sung out-of-tune as a reinforcement of how useless they are, and will retreat further into their hiding place.

3. Not taking enough care in listening

Over the years I have met so many people who don't know how to listen. They're just a bit careless. I don't mean to sound disrespectful toward them – it's not their fault. They just don't realise that music is more precision-based than they think, and that you have to take care in trying to match the notes. They imagine that it's a bit like talking. For example, when you ask a question, you often go up in pitch at the end, but it doesn't matter how much. That depends on how high or low your voice is, how interested you are, what your regional accent dictates, and all sorts of other things. But with singing, you have to be more precise. It's not enough to be vaguely *near* the destination note. You have to be *on* it, otherwise it sounds wrong.

4. Not knowing which muscles to move

Sometimes people can hear that they're not singing the right note, but they don't know what to do to change it. They literally don't know how to control those muscles, especially with fine motor movements. A common response that I get to the instruction 'a little bit higher' is someone singing the same note but a little bit louder. You have to get to know what it feels like to move up or down in pitch a little bit or a lot. It's like when you first go to a Pilates class: 'How do I move that muscle? I didn't even know it existed!' You have to learn which bits of your body to move in order to make the pitch go higher or lower. This is likely to resonate with many of you. If you're thinking 'This is me', there is hope! You can learn to do this.

5. Playing it safe

This is really common. Some people do not trust their voice in a higher register, so they stick to familiar territory (ie, their speaking voice, which is usually quite low in your range). Lots of people simply aren't confident in their upper register, and thus they stay in the safe zone where they know they have some degree of control. They're just not sure what notes will come out if they sing up there, so they don't try.

Just a reminder
I want to take this opportunity to remind you of something important. I am an expert in this. Your parent, or sibling, or teacher, or school friend, or school bully,

who laughed at you or who singled you out for not being able to hit the correct notes **was not qualified** to make that judgement. They may have been correct in having told you (however kindly or unkindly) that you were not hitting those notes, but they were not qualified to make the judgement that you are unable to sing, or to learn to sing, as a result. I am qualified to make that decision. My expertise trumps theirs.

I'm not saying this to puff up my own sense of self-importance. I'm saying it so that I can make it easier for you to change your mindset. It's science, really. We can hold irrational beliefs about something, but hopefully, if we're intelligent, we can change our minds once we're presented with enough evidence to the contrary. I need you to believe that I'm very knowledgeable about what I do, and very well-qualified to debunk some of the myths that you have just assumed to be true over the years.

TLDR

- Lack of confidence is a huge barrier to singing.

- This lack of confidence can have many sources.

- The parents, schoolteachers, siblings and friends who told you that you can't sing were talking out of ignorance.

- Singing teachers often don't realise that it's nearly always possible to teach someone to pitch.

- I am an expert in this – believe me, not them.

- Most people who sing don't get it right a lot of the time, but because they're not worried about their voices, they just shrug and try to do it better the next time.

- **Most often, the only difference between a 'singer' and a 'non-singer' is their attitude to getting it wrong** (I know I said that earlier but it's worth repeating).

- It's highly likely that you don't take enough care in listening and trying to match the note.

- It's also likely that you don't know which muscles to move, and actually *how* to tune notes so that they're slightly higher or lower.

— It's also very possible that on the rare occasions that you sing, you stay within a comfort zone of a tiny range of notes, simply because you don't trust the notes that might come out of your mouth if you move outside that.

Go and watch the next couple of videos. The first one will give you a little more practice in pitching random notes. It's a short video, but you can replay it over again just to make sure you can get the notes it asks for:

 https://lcv.pub/TYCSTA04

The second one focuses on a technique called swooping. This is helpful if you find yourself struggling to hit a note accurately. If you approach the note with a swoop at the beginning, you're much more likely to hit it. As you get more practised, you can reduce the amount of swoop that you put in, until you can hit it without any need for swooping at all:

 https://lcv.pub/TYCSTA05

When you've finished there, go on to the next chapter, **Control**.

CONTROL

I want you to let yourself off the hook. I want you to give yourself an easier time of it. Many of you probably feel that it's ridiculous that you can't sing. You feel that you constantly fail in a task that even small children can do. You feel that you ought to be able to do this, that it's such a basic human capability, that you're somehow deficient because you can't. And here's the thing: it's partly because you think that the task should be so easy that you don't succeed at it. Let me explain.

that's nice

While it's true that lots of children can sing, seemingly very naturally from a very early age, it's certainly not always the case. But they can usually learn. (I say 'usually', as I obviously haven't investigated every case here.) I had two sibling piano pupils some years ago. They were seven and nine years old. Both of them were extremely musical and very keen. The youngest wanted to learn to play piano while she sang, and she was a great singer – very accurate. The eldest was much more accomplished on the piano, but much less accurate as a singer at first. I would encourage her to sing along, and she would sometimes sing totally different notes from where she was supposed to be. It took a little while for this to improve, but the key to this was gentle encouragement, like 'Hang on, let's get that starting note right', '...bit higher... even more... there we are.' The two worst things I could have done there would have been (a) to say, 'That's terrible, you're really flat! Maybe you shouldn't sing!' or (b) ignored the wrong notes and allowed her to carry on singing the wrong notes. If you're teaching a child an activity, normally you encourage and praise lots, but you also correct the wrong things and show how to do them properly.

keep pedalling!

keep going!

Things children are encouraged to do but when done incorrectly, gently corrected and shown how to do better	Things children are told they're simply incapable of doing when they don't do it well
Hold a pencil	
Brush their teeth	
Swim	
Ski	Sing
Play tennis	
Draw	
Play the piano	
Do gymnastics	
Cook	
Sew	
Wash themselves	
Hold a knife and fork	
Manage money	
Use a knife to chop vegetables	
Posture	
Use chopsticks	
Behave	
Use a potter's wheel	
Ride a bike	
Ballet dance	
Use a pair of scissors	
Dance	
Handwriting	
Martial arts	
Whistling	
Throwing a ball	
Tying a tie or shoelace	
Correct grip for various sports	

Let me explain why you shouldn't feel bad about not being naturally able to sing. Believe it or not, singing does not come naturally to any of us. It is a learned behaviour. It may be learned really early in life, but it is learned nonetheless. When you think about it, singing is quite a complicated process. Your brain has to decode the vibrations that your ear is hearing, then either measure or predict the frequency that you are going to have to recreate with your voice. Then it needs to make the necessary muscular shifts to enable that to happen, all within a split second. And this is a vast simplification of the process. In order for all this to happen subconsciously, a certain amount of muscle memory is required.

We teach children the muscle movements for the items in the left column above, which then, after enough practice, become stored (we believe) in the basal ganglia (ie, muscle memory). I'll go into the whole area of muscle memory in a bit more detail later in the book.

Let's drill down some more here. When we model to children how to do these things, what we're actually asking them to do first is construct those actions in their minds, before they carry them out. You may have never thought about it this way before, but when we learn a skill, we have to imagine ourselves doing that activity correctly before we actually put that action into practice, and we can then associate that correct movement with the mental image.

This is how actions can be stored in the memory. If those things never enter the muscle memory, the brain doesn't have the frame of reference to be able to say, 'This feels right/wrong.'

you've almost tied a bow

If you're reading this book, you're likely to be someone who was never particularly encouraged to sing. That may be because you weren't very accurate with your pitching as a child, so you were written off as tone-deaf.

Alternatively, it may be that there simply wasn't lots of music around as you were growing up, and for one reason or another, you didn't exercise your voice. Whatever the reason, you probably don't have these reference points stored in your head, nor any organised way of accessing them. You may like listening to music, but you also probably have no idea how melody actually works.

There are people who can drive a manual car, and there are people who can't. Those of you who can, I want you to think back to your first driving lesson. You probably had both feet on the pedals, and then your instructor would have asked you to gently lift your foot off the clutch. Now, because you didn't really know how to control your foot at that stage, you did what you thought was correct. What you thought was a small movement was, in fact, quite a big one, and the car would have lurched forward. It took you some time to get used to the small movements – the fine motor skills. Later on, as you acclimatise to what it feels like to perform smaller movements of the foot, this is no longer an issue and is just something that you do automatically.

The point I'm making here is that despite not yet having this experience, and never having learned before, I suspect that most of you would have no problem believing that you would be able to learn if you decided to put your mind to it. It's the same with singing. You have to be prepared to spend some time learning the fine motor skills required, but once you do, you'll find it easy.

TLDR

- Part of the reason you don't succeed in singing accurately is probably because you think it should come naturally.

- **Singing does not come *naturally* to anyone – it is learned behaviour.**

- You shouldn't feel silly because you're not very accurate with pitching.

- Singing is quite a complicated series of processes, which is modelled to most people in childhood.

- If you weren't taught this as a child, you will have to learn the process as an adult.

- Singing involves fine motor skills which have to be practised.

Head over to the website now, and watch the video about accuracy. It's a bit like some of the previous videos, but with more notes to hit:

 https://lcv.pub/TYCSTAo6

EEK!

5

BOTH EASIER AND HARDER THAN YOU THINK

I want to build on something I mentioned in the last chapter. Singing is both way more complicated and much easier than you think it is. Let me explain that slightly contradictory statement.

How is singing harder than I think it is?

Well, it's a matter of perception. Bear with me here. You have to understand a whole other perspective. And keep reading, because there is proper hope if you can understand how this works.

As I mentioned earlier, many of you think that singing *should* be easy, because lots of small children can do it, seemingly effortlessly and without instruction. What you're not taking on board is that those children *have* had instruction – it's just disguised as little games and things which go unnoticed, like Mummy singing 'The Wheels on the Bus'. If Mummy didn't think much of her own voice, and never sang to you, that's hours and hours of missed lessons right there. If you were discouraged from singing from an early age, there will be hours of practising that other people have had that you haven't.

So nowadays, when you do try to sing, *because* you think it should be easy, and *because* you see others doing it effortlessly and naturally, you attempt to do so as if you had the training that they have had, without first establishing those muscle memories – those neural connections.

How is it easier than I think it is?

It's time for some home truths. You're holding yourself to much too high a standard. As I've said before, most people aren't amazing singers, neither do they think they are. They're just confident that they can hold a tune most or all of the time. They don't think they're going to be the next X-Factor star. They might or might not think they're capable of delivering a solo, but they're probably confident enough to sing 'Happy Birthday' or sing karaoke at the pub. They will happily accept that they'll go wrong sometimes and that their technique needs a lot of work. They will sing casually, without thinking they're amazing, in the same way that they might go running without thinking they may do a marathon, or play five-a-side football without feeling that they might be picked for a professional team. I can confidently say that the majority of you reading this book are perfectly capable of easily learning to sing in that 'amateur' league – *you just need to be able to accept that you'll do it imperfectly, like most of the world does.*

Some of you cringe inwardly and outwardly when you hear your own voice. There's simply no need. So often I have someone tell me, 'I'm terrible at singing, my voice is awful', and when I finally persuade them to sing me something, they're absolutely fine – a little wavery here and there, but completely adequate for a choir, for example. There's this perception that there always has to be a judgement about how well someone does something, like you're on show. This famous quote, attributed to Kurt Vonnegut but actually written by THREE--RINGS on tumblr, sums it up nicely:

❚❚ *When I was 15 I spent a month working on an archeological dig. I was talking to one of the archeologists one day during our lunch break and he asked those kinds of 'getting to know you' questions you ask young people: Do you play sports? What's your favorite subject? And I told him, no I don't play any sports. I do theater, I'm in choir, I play the violin and piano, I used to take art classes.*

And he went WOW. That's amazing! And I said, 'Oh no, but I'm not any good at ANY of them.'

And he said something then that I will never forget and which absolutely blew my mind because no one had ever said anything like it to me before: 'I don't think being good at things is the point of doing them. I think you've got all these wonderful experiences with different skills, and that all teaches you things and makes you an interesting person, no matter how well you do them.'

And that honestly changed my life. Because I went from a failure, someone who hadn't been talented enough at anything to excel, to someone who did things because I enjoyed them. I had been raised in such an achievement-oriented environment, so inundated with the myth of Talent, that I thought it was only worth doing things if you could 'Win' at them. **II**

A story, to help you understand

At the time of writing this, I'm 53 years old. When I grew up, we didn't have much money. Enough to send me to piano lessons, but certainly not enough to do any of the nice trips that my school organised. Consequently, I never learned to ski as a child. Never thinking of myself as a particularly sporty person either, it's not something I was drawn to, and for one reason or another, I got to the age of 48 before I decided to go skiing. It was actually a skiing trip that we organised for a group from my choir, London City Voices. We figured that we'd attract a larger variety of people on the trip if we made it clear that some of us in the leadership had never been skiing before. I was supposed to go to a day-long training session at a snow centre before the trip, but I developed shingles and had to cancel. The result of this was that just a few years ago I found myself in Borovets, Bulgaria, in my first ever beginner class, learning to shuffle across what felt like a really steep slope (actually about five degrees) wearing a pair of skis.

Now, this slope was actually the very last bit of a red slope, just where it completely flattens out. There were a fair few people hurtling down it at speed from time-to-time. Many of these were small children, who would have been learning to ski for as long as they could walk.

Would it have been sensible to assume that because these children were able to ski so proficiently, that I ought to be able to do the same thing? Perhaps I should just have taken the ski-lift up to the top of the red slope and flung myself down, trusting that because most of the other people there could do it easily, it would come naturally to me too?

That would have been crazy.

Instead, I humbled myself, tried to copy my instructor, fell over a lot, got it wrong, made progress, fell over more, took some risks, more falling over, more risks, slightly less falling over, and finally came out at the end of the week with a fairly stable skiing technique. Here's a video of me at the end of five days of instruction, with a bit of a surprise ending (they didn't tell us that there was a school skiing gala taking place that day):

 https://lcv.pub/TYCSTA-SKI

Five years on and I'm a reasonable skier. I can get down a black slope if it's not too icy. I'm never going to win any prizes for it, but that's not why I do it. I do it because I enjoy it, and actually, I really like the fact that I came to it quite late in life but am now reasonably competent.

This story does a few things. It shows how you can learn things later in life and still really enjoy doing them. It shows that you don't have to always do things brilliantly, and that you can be amateurish about them and it's fine. But really, the point of it is that I had to put myself through a learning curve and get the basics established before really going for it. I had to submit to tutoring in the essentials, and allow myself to be wrong. I had to hear the words 'no, not quite like that' repeatedly, without telling myself that I was rubbish or allowing myself to become disheartened. I had to tell myself 'I can do this' many, many times, when I felt like I couldn't, and when three-year-olds were gracefully and fearlessly slipping past me.

TLDR

- Singing is easier than you think it is.

- Singing is also more complicated than you think it is.

- These two apparently contradictory statements are both true.

- Most 'singing-avoiders' think that people who are comfortable with singing are much more accurate than they actually are.

- People who were musically nurtured as children have thousands of hours of instruction (disguised as games, songs, etc) in their past, which you may not have.

- There is a parallel with coming to skiing (or in fact any skill) later in life.

- There is a learning curve that you have to go through, including learning the basics.

- You may not get it right straightaway – in fact it might take some time, and hard work.

Do you see? Is this making sense? I'm sure you can see the parallel here. You're going to have to learn the absolute basics before you can do this without thinking. So, you're going to have to put a bit of work in, and be prepared to be corrected here and there without throwing in the towel. Let me show you where to start. Move straight on to the next chapter, and I'll give you an exercise when you've read that.

AIMING

You may not realise this, but singing is a precision sport. I think that sometimes people who aren't used to singing see more experienced people singing quite effortlessly, and so they don't realise the amount of effort that goes into aiming for a note.

In my choir, London City Voices, we have new people joining most weeks. Lots of those new people may not have done much (or any) singing in their life so far. Sometimes they don't sing the right notes. Nine times out of ten, they're not singing high enough. When I notice this, I first try out a few general techniques, such as getting everyone to sing loudly and confidently, but this doesn't always work. If it doesn't, I'll catch them at the end, and ask if they mind if I try to help them a little. I'll usually say that I'd noticed that they weren't always able to access some of the higher notes, and I'd like to give them a mini-lesson to help them. We'll wait till everybody's gone, so they're not embarrassed. I then say to them, 'Sing me this note', and I'll sing a note to them. Almost invariably what happens is, instead of waiting to hear the note that I want them to sing, they just sing any old note. They haven't even had time to process the pitch, even if they knew how to. To be clear, if an experienced singer came in as early as that, they might not get it right either because there hasn't been enough time for the brain to process the note.

Usually, when that happens, I stop them, explain why, and ask them to listen while I sing it a couple of times, then to try again. Often they'll get it right that time. If they don't, I'll pitch the note they just sang, and get them to repeat it, so they can hear both of us singing it. Then I'll do another note, close to the one they just sang, and see if they can match that. We cover a lot of this in my one-to-one coaching sessions.

The reason that people often come in so quickly is that they are keen to show willing, and they think that it's important to respond immediately, so they leap in with a random guess. They just go for a note and hope that it's the right one. You can't do that with music. You have to aim.

Aiming in music is all about listening. Listening is the first, and arguably the most important aspect of getting the pitch right when it comes to singing. Listening is not the same as hearing. Hearing is a passive activity, listening is a deliberate one. When you're trying to sing the same note as somebody else, you have to make a concerted effort to really match the pitch. I'll come to the second aspect of pitching in a moment, but it's important to note that you may never have realised that you have to aim.

Let's say you're on a shooting range and you've got a target in front of you. If you just point the gun in some random direction, pull the trigger and hope for the best, you're not going to be very accurate. You have to actually make a conscious decision to aim at the target – to point the gun in the right direction, to look down the barrel, try to predict where the bullet will go, and then pull the trigger. That's how it works. If you're on a football field, you have to aim at the goal. Your brain has to do some calculations in order to predict where the ball will go. You can't just kick anywhere you like and hope that it might go in the goal. It doesn't work like that. It's the same with the voice. You have to learn how to aim, and lots of people don't know how to do that, or don't even realise that it's necessary.

If you grew up in a household where music was all around you all the time then it's more likely that you'll find it easier to pitch effortlessly. Having said that, it's not necessarily a given. It's definitely more likely that if there wasn't much music around you in your childhood, you'll find it harder to pitch.

Here's a good example of where people often fail to aim in singing. I asked a student of mine to record himself singing a tune which repeated the same note many times in a row. He got the note to start with, but he stopped paying attention to it, so the result was that it dropped in pitch. He stopped concentrating, he got complacent, and then he went **flat** (lower in pitch than he should have been). So, I decided to write him a song, and now you get to use that too. It's called 'Stay On It'. Pop over to the website now and try it. As with one of the earlier lessons, I've made two videos, one for low voices and one for high voices:

LOW VOICES

https://lcv.pub/TYCSTA07low

HIGH VOICES

https://lcv.pub/TYCSTA07high

It's a fun exercise, and it may take you some time to get the hang of. There's proper singing in this one. Then come back here and finish this chapter.

You've probably heard the phrase 'practice makes perfect' before. I'm not sure that it always makes perfect, but it certainly makes a good deal better.

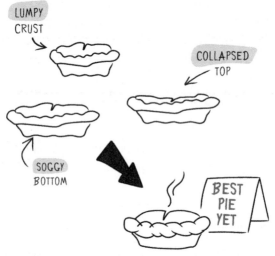

I'm sure there are many things that you do in your daily life that you are much better at now simply because you've spent time trying to do them more accurately or efficiently. I've already mentioned driving. With cooking or baking, you learn exactly how much oil to add, or what to look for to check that something's cooked or not. In your job there will be things that you do much better and more efficiently now than when you first started. You learn what works and what doesn't, and over time you (hopefully) do more of the things that work and less of the ones that don't. You're going to have to go through this process with singing. And in order to do this, you're going to have to become what I call an **Honest Self-Critic**.

TLDR

- Singing is a precision sport.

- You have to consciously aim at the note.

- In order to aim, you have to *learn how* to aim.

- Aiming involves making a conscious decision to match the pitch.

- You have to keep on consciously aiming – you can't just stop doing it.

- In order to get better at aiming, you have to learn what you're not doing correctly in order to be able to improve.

THE HONEST SELF-CRITIC

Being an Honest Self-Critic (HSC) is a really useful skill in general life, not just learning to sing. It requires a degree of security in oneself, but even if you don't feel particularly secure, just try and put some of this into play and you'll be amazed how much it will positively affect your outlook.

It's important to note that the word 'critic' in the term 'self-critic' doesn't imply negativity. It just means being fully reflective about the way you evaluate your ability. Being a self-critic doesn't mean that you constantly tell yourself, 'I'm terrible at that particular thing.' Instead, it means that you ask yourself honestly, 'How am I really doing at this? What am I doing well? What things could I improve, and how?'

Traits of an Honest Self–Critic

Accepting mistakes, rather than exaggerating or creating unnecessary drama

An HSC doesn't go off in a sulk when they get something wrong. They don't throw their toys out of the pram when they don't do something perfectly. Instead, they try to learn what it is that's wrong about the way they did the thing, and they make the decision to try and implement that the next time they attempt the task.

Being realistic rather than writing themselves off

An HSC believes that they are capable of learning how to do a thing. They listen to common sense, and they don't hold irrational beliefs about themselves, such as 'I have the worst voice in the world', 'I have no co-ordination skills', 'I'm just a failure'. They're happy to bow to the expertise of people who are accomplished in the activity, and to accept that while they may not be able to do a thing yet, given sufficient expert tuition and practice, they will be able to succeed in their goal of improving at said activity. An HSC will accept evidence when it presents itself. For example, if there is clear evidence of improvement (or not) in an activity, the HSC will accept this and adjust their practice to reflect this.

Adopting a positive attitude to mistakes

This really is something that can apply to the whole of life, and it's fairly easy to learn how to do it, if you're willing. An HSC will take the view that a mistake is simply an opportunity to learn how to do something better, rather than despising themselves for making that mistake.

Here's another anecdote for you. Some years ago, I was teaching private piano lessons to adults. I had one student – let's call her Mary. She was really musical and was making some progress, but this progress was hampered because of a particular behaviour pattern. Every time she played a wrong note, she had a visceral reaction to it. She jumped almost as if she'd been burned. The result was that she was almost scared to play any of the notes in case they were wrong ones. I had to teach her to love her mistakes. 'But why would you love your mistakes?!' I hear you protest. Because they show you how not to do it. There's the saying attributed to Thomas Edison regarding the invention of the electric lightbulb that he had 'not failed 10,000 times, just found 10,000 ways that won't work'. Knowing what you did wrong, in order that you don't repeat your mistake, is a really important part of learning. I mentioned my late development as a skier earlier on in this book. In order to become a better skier, it is important that I know what it feels like (and what happens) if, for example, I put my weight on the back of the ski instead of the front, when heading down a hill. Making that mistake is quite important, in order that you don't keep on making it. Obviously, if you don't learn from those mistakes, that's quite a different thing, but it's really important to seize mistakes as a learning opportunity.

SPOT OPPORTUNITY

This goes hand-in-hand with the previous point, about not writing oneself off. If you decide to learn a new skill, I have to tell you that **you will make mistakes!** You will get things wrong, probably lots of times. Your attitude to how you approach these errors will massively affect the progress you make. If you give up when you make a mistake, you simply won't learn anything. These mistakes are a really important part of the learning process.

FORGET UNTRUTHS

Accepting praise

An HSC learns how to accept honest praise, particularly from teachers or people who are more advanced than them. Don't assume that people are saying nice things to you that they don't mean just to make you feel better. Assume that if they give you a compliment, they mean it. This is something that lots of people struggle with due to poor self-image. However, it's worth saying that if you are complimented by people who know about the activity that you're learning, and you decide not to accept what they are saying, it's not very polite. You are essentially telling them that you don't think their judgement is correct.

Try to adopt these traits when you go about learning to sing. Allow yourself to be corrected without taking umbrage. Don't be offended when people try politely to help you with making a better sound. Lay aside the unhelpful and untrue myths about how bad you are. Aim to learn from your mistakes. Finally, accept praise where it is due from people who matter.

TLDR

- In order to improve, you have to be *honestly self-critical*.

- This doesn't mean telling yourself that you're terrible.

- It means being honest about whether you did something well or not.

- You have to learn to love your mistakes, as they teach you what you did wrong.

- You have to learn to accept correction from people who can teach you.

- You have to learn to accept praise from people who are qualified to judge.

- Ignore the unhelpful voices in your head, telling you that you can't do it.

- You have to accept that *you will make mistakes*, and that they're essential for the learning process.

Check out my short video on this on the website. Then come back and go to the next chapter, **Being Fully Present and Aware**:

 https://lcv.pub/TYCSTA08

8

BEING FULLY PRESENT AND AWARE

Let's move on to the next thing that will help you to improve your singing: being fully present and aware. This sounds like a pretentious title for a chapter, doesn't it! What do I mean when I say 'fully present and aware'?

I'm going to carry on with my skiing analogy, as it works so well. If you watched my little video that I shared earlier, you'll have seen an example of me not being fully present and aware. If not, it's here:

https://lcv.pub/TYCSTA-SKI

Watch until the end.

By that stage I had learned the basics of skiing, enough to navigate myself down an easy blue run. However, I hadn't yet learned the importance of keeping my wits about me in order to spot changing circumstances or, indeed, what might be lying just ahead. The mechanics of staying upright and going forward are important when skiing, but so is knowing who else is around you and what sort of hazards you might encounter.

There are all kinds of circumstances in which you might find yourself singing. Perhaps it's singing hymns at a wedding or Midnight Mass. Perhaps you want to join a choir. Maybe you're at karaoke, or a big singalong in a pub, or perhaps you're on the terraces at a football match. Maybe you're just singing 'Happy Birthday' to a friend when they bring out the cake with the candles. Whatever the circumstances, you need to be aware of what else is happening around you, and what your role is in the proceedings.

Let me give you some examples. Let's say you've joined a choir. Generally, choirs sing in parts, according to voice type. There will be different parts to sing, depending on how high or low the natural pitch of your voice is. You might be a tenor – generally a high male voice (or a very low female voice). You will be expected to sing the same part as the other tenors, while deliberately not singing the same parts as the other voices (normally soprano, alto and bass). This means that you have to tune your ear into what the tenors are singing so that you don't inadvertently sing the wrong part.

If everyone sings the right bits, the harmony (the blend of the different notes together) should work. It sometimes takes a little while to get the hang of this, but if you struggle, try and sit yourself in the middle of your section at the front, so you're surrounded by the correct notes. Alternatively, plonk yourself next to someone who you know to be a strong singer (ask for a recommendation if necessary). Also, a good tip is to make yourself accountable immediately by introducing yourself and saying something along the lines of 'Hi there – I'm sometimes not very sure of my pitching, so if you wouldn't mind helping me out by giving me an indication when I'm singing the wrong notes, I'd really appreciate it.' This is a great way of taking away that feeling of awkwardness, because you've given people permission to correct you without causing offence.

Bad Karaoke

Let's say you've psyched yourself up to sing karaoke at the pub. The expectation here is not that you sing the same as anyone else, as there's probably no one else singing with you. However, you have to listen to the backing track and make sure that you're (a) in sync with the timing, and (b) starting on the correct note. You can't just start on any note. Well, you can, but it won't sound right unless you start on the right one. I have listened to so many karaoke performances at the pub where the singer sounds terrible, simply because they haven't been fully present and aware enough to take the time to start on the right note, and then they've continued singing at that pitch without trying to correct themselves.

Check out this video, which demonstrates this for you in detail.

https://lcv.pub/TYCSTA09

To use an analogy, singing without taking care of which note you're starting on is a bit like someone making a cake, but not noticing or caring that they put 150g of salt in instead of sugar. It just requires a bit of attention to detail to correct this mistake. Some of this often goes by the wayside because of the self-deprecation that I mentioned in a previous chapter. People actually make the conscious choice not to care, because they feel they are so bad at singing that it becomes a joke. It almost defines them. The best singer in the world will also sound appalling if they sing a karaoke song starting on the wrong note (assuming they don't adjust).

So, how do we become fully present and aware? There's a simple answer. Focus.

What's the difference between being **fully present and aware** and **focus**?

The first is a state which you need to attain. The second is what you need to actually do to attain this state. Have you ever driven or walked somewhere, then when you arrived, you have no real memory of the journey? You were switched off, or on auto-pilot. One part of your brain was functioning enough for you to complete the actions required to get you there, but you weren't really present. I find this happens more and more these days when I'm following my satnav. My brain isn't really engaging with the directions, and if I were asked to retrace that route, there's a very good chance that I wouldn't be able to. The same can happen when we're singing. We do whatever we've always done, with whatever accuracy that entails, and we're not paying attention to all those external factors which we really should be doing in order to sound right.

The problem with drummers

I have played in many bands over the years, and recorded many drummers. I've spotted something that I believe not many people notice. The ability to hit certain drums in a particular order and the ability to stay solidly in time with an external stimulus are not necessarily part of the same skillset. What do I mean? Well, in short, it means that just because you can play the drums doesn't mean that you're good at keeping time. They are completely different skills. You ought to be good at both, if you really consider yourself to be a drummer, but I can tell you for a fact that there are a lot of drummers out there who have spent a lot of time learning to hit things in the right order, but who really have not developed their sense of timing very well. Essentially, they get faster or slower during a song, when they're supposed to keep the tempo consistent. In order to keep time properly, a drummer has to focus, to be constantly asking, 'Am I getting faster/slower?' to the point where it becomes second nature.

I used to record demo tracks for young bands, and once I had a trio come in and record in my studio. The drummer absolutely could not stay in time with the guide click track, to the point where I had to send them out to lunch, then find a single bar of the drummer's track that was in time, and copy/paste it over and over. The point I am making here is that these out-of-time drummers are not allowing themselves to be fully present and aware. They are not synchronising with the other things that are going on in the music, as they think that they are the ones with whom everyone else has to synchronise. This is true to a point, in that bands should use the drums as their metronome, but only if the drummer is in time themselves. Drummers have to be open to the possibility that they may go out of time, and focusing to make sure this doesn't happen. Unfortunately, pride gets in the way with lots of them. I've worked with drummers who have been mortally offended at the suggestion that they may have speeded up or slowed down during the song.

So, if even trained musicians sometimes lack this awareness of their propensity to get things wrong, you, as a newcomer to this skill, have to be open to the likelihood that you might not always be focusing on the right things, and start to work out how to do so.

The good news is that it's possible to go from a state of non-awareness to one of total presence, if you learn what to look for. It's a bit like if someone draws attention to a new fashion item, or a particular model of bicycle, you suddenly start to notice them everywhere, having been totally unaware of their existence before. These little details in music can hide in plain sight until someone points them out to you, then you'll begin to be aware of them.

TLDR

- You have to learn to be aware of what else is going on in the music.

- Put yourself in situations that allow you to succeed, eg, surrounding yourself with strong singers.

- If you're in a choir, make yourself accountable, so that people feel they can gently correct you when you don't hit the right notes.

- Take the time to check things like the starting note. And really check them – don't just pretend to do so.

- Every song is in a particular key, or set of notes. It's important to establish in your head what that set of notes is before starting to sing the song, and make sure that you're in the same key as any other musicians or the backing track.

- 'Happy Birthday' is often a good example of when this doesn't happen.

- You have to keep checking to make sure that you're still in key. *This never stops!*

Take yourself over to the website and learn my little blues song. You're going to sing it in several different keys, and you're going to learn how to listen to the backing in a way that will inform the starting note that you choose. Again, there are two videos for this lesson, one for low voices and one for high voices. When you're done, move on to the next chapter, where I'm going to tell you about the peculiar nature of 'Happy Birthday':

LOW VOICES

https://lcv.pub/TYCSTA1olow

HIGH VOICES

https://lcv.pub/TYCSTA1ohigh

PAY
ATTENTION

LISTEN
CAREFULLY

FOCUS

NOTE CORRECTIONS

KNOW THE
KEY

KEEP IN
TIME

BE NEAR
STRONG
SINGERS

THE PHENOMENON OF 'HAPPY BIRTHDAY'

The most common failure to be fully present and aware during singing is simply during the song 'Happy Birthday'. There's a funny psychological phenomenon that happens with 'Happy Birthday', depending on the people involved. But before I explain that, I need to explain the concept of **musical key** to you.

A very basic definition of **key** when talking about music, could be 'the set of notes used to sing or play a piece of music'. Essentially, if there is no backing music, you can start a song on any note, and as long as you use the same distances between the notes, it will sound right. An analogy (you'll notice that I like analogies) is that you can draw a square anywhere – as long as you draw length X, turn 90 degrees and do the same three more times, you'll end up with a square.

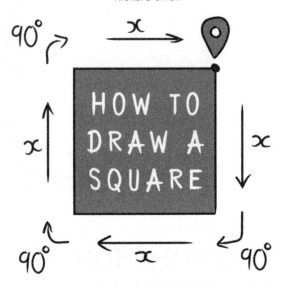

If three different people draw three squares, and they all start at the same point and use the same lengths, they'll end up with three squares which line up with each other.

If they don't start at the same point, those three squares will not line up.

So, if three different people sing or play that piece of music starting on the same note, it will sound right.

If one or more of them start on a different note and continue to sing like that, the notes will sound wrong.

If you've ever watched any episodes of *Only Connect* (a BBC quiz show of which I am a huge fan), there are often excruciating moments (which is kind of the point really) where the host, Victoria Coren-Mitchell, gets the teams to sing a well-known chorus of a song, totally unaccompanied, with nothing more than '1, 2, 3, (4)' as an intro. It's totally hit and miss. On occasion there's someone fairly strong to lead, but often the team members are totally embarrassed and don't know what they're doing, so they all start on different notes, and the resulting sound is quite... special... see the link for an example:

 https://lcv.pub/TYCSTA-OC

With 'Happy Birthday', if it's a group of musicians singing, or there's a musician there, one person will usually give the starting note to make sure that everyone is singing the right tune. Sometimes, some of them might sing alternative tunes which make it sound even nicer (harmony).

If it's not a group of musicians, sometimes there is a more confident person who sings loudly and other people align their pitch to that person. Sometimes there's nobody very confident to lead, so everyone just bumbles along at various pitches and with varying degrees of accuracy. The result of this means that 'Happy Birthday' can sometimes sound amazing and sometimes terrible.

CHECK THE KEY

SET OF NOTES USED TO PLAY OR SING A PIECE OF MUSIC

Lots of people aren't fully present and aware during 'Happy Birthday', which is what leads to it often sounding terrible. If everyone starts in a different key but then is sufficiently aware to correct themselves, it'll start off sounding awful, then there will be this weird fleeting moment when everyone is adjusting and then suddenly it'll be fine. Obviously, you have no control over what other people do, but if you want to be fully present and aware during this, you can decide to listen to another person and try and match their pitch. This mixture of abilities while singing a song together is actually quite a strange phenomenon, and yet this song gets sung spontaneously by diverse groups of people millions of times a day all over the world.

That's not all though. There's something else that happens in the song. Let me break it down for you, line by line.

Happy birthday to you
Happy birthday to you
Happy birthday dear Richard
Happy birthday to you

Now let's see what those words look like if we assign a height to each of them according to their pitch.

I'll sing it again.

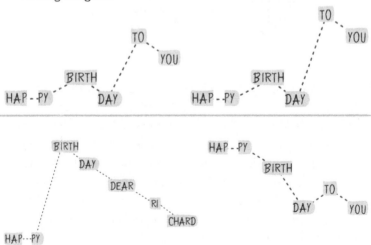

There are two things about this tune that cause issues. The first is that the first two lines are *almost* the same but *not quite*. There's a slight difference between them but it's quite easy to miss.

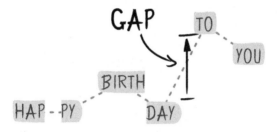

So you've got 'to you' and then 'to you'. Both have the same shape (pair of notes, where the first of the pair is higher than the second), but the second 'to you' is situated slightly higher than the first.

The second thing is that there's quite a large leap in pitch in the third line.

This gap is the one that causes the main problem. People are scared to take that risk in jumping a gap that large. They think something along the lines of, 'I don't know what my voice might sound like up there, so I'm not even going to try.'

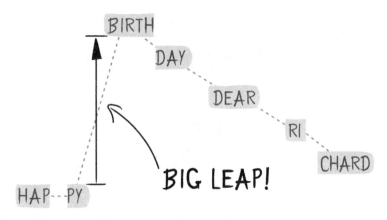

The combination of those two things leads to a performance of 'Happy Birthday' sounding and looking more like this:

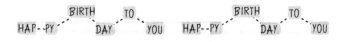

I've explained all this in lots of detail in my video, so do have a watch. I've used some animation to show you how all the stuff above works. You'll also get to see some before-and-after video of some of my students singing 'Happy Birthday', after just a very short time spent with me. This shows you how quickly you can make progress when you have a teacher who can identify what it is you're doing wrong, and who can explain how you can fix that:

https://lcv.pub/TYCSTA11

When you've watched this and understood it, turn to the next chapter. I'm going to show you some music theory.

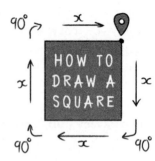

HOW TO PITCH HAPPY BIRTHDAY

REQUIRED

A HAPPY BIRTHDAY TO YOU

B HAPPY BIRTHDAY DEAR SOMEONE

STEP 1

GAP

A HAP - PY BIRTH DAY TO YOU

STEP 2

BIGGER GAP

A HAP - PY BIRTH DAY TO YOU

STEP 3

B HAP - PY BIRTH DAY DEAR SOME ONE

BIG LEAP!

BE CONFIDENT AIM HIGH GO FOR IT!

STEP 4

A HAP - PY BIRTH DAY TO YOU

STAY HIGHER

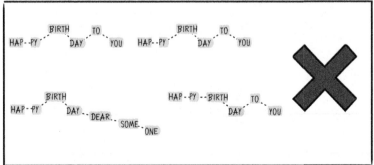

SOME USEFUL THEORY

Music is an unusual blend of art and science. Sound and pitch are obviously made up of waveforms and frequency, hence science, but the way the notes are arranged and then delivered is the art form. It's useful to understand the science.

Don't freeze up and glaze over because you remember how boring your music lessons were at school. It's important to know how this works, and if you've read this far you're completely capable of taking this in. Yes, it's a bit tricky to understand at first. However, stick with me. I've done you a marvellous video to accompany this chapter, because I know this is the bit that people zone out on. Read the chapter, watch the video, read the chapter again. It'll make sense to you. Even if you don't get it completely at the beginning, reading it and then watching the video will make a difference to how you perceive music. The link to the video is at the end of the chapter.

Pitch, and the names of notes

Pitch is simply how high or low a note sounds. Scientifically, we speak about **frequency**, which sounds odd at first, because frequency means how often something occurs. So, how this works is as follows: the reason it's called frequency is that it is to do with how many times a second a waveform occurs, which affects the pitch that we perceive the note to have. Notes that sound higher in **pitch** have a waveform that happens more times a second (therefore have a higher **frequency**) than notes that sound lower.

Think of a ramp, where the bottom of the ramp represents a low note, and the top of the ramp represents (surprise!) a high note. You could convert that ramp into equal steps, breaking up the continuous line into specific points. That's what notes are – just specific points along the continuous line of pitch.

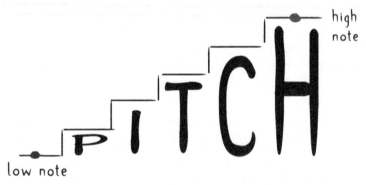

Those points have absolute frequencies, and over the years a system has been developed that most of the western world uses. In this system, certain absolute pitches (frequencies) are given simplified names. These names are the first seven letters of the alphabet, and then certain frequencies in between these seven notes have a sort of 'dual nationality'. These in-between notes are named according to the two notes that they are next to. So, there is a space for a note between the notes C and D. We call this note either C# (C-sharp) or Db (D-flat). The note produced when a waveform cycles at 440Hz is A, specifically the A that is slightly to the right of the middle of a piano keyboard (also known as A4).

There's a lot that could be said here about the history, but it's not essential for you right now. What is essential to know is that within most Western musical traditions, this musical slide-rule has 12 subdivisions, which are then repeated over and over again. The similarly-named notes sound like higher or lower versions of themselves. These notes go from A0 (lowest) to G8 (highest). Obviously, you can go infinitely high and low, but A0-G8 is about the limit that's useful to music, so we generally stop measuring there.

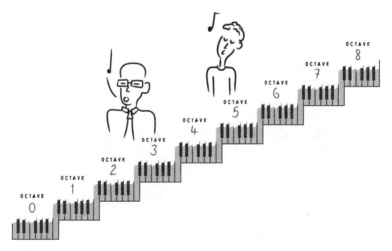

These extreme ends are pretty low and high, so we'll be more used to hearing notes between about A1 and G7. So, A3 (12 notes below A4) and A5 (12 notes above) have similarities with each other. If you play an A on a piano (any A) to, for example, a man with a very deep voice and a boy with a high voice and ask them both to sing that note, they will probably sing different versions of A, but most people will be able to hear that the notes are related, or similar to each other in some way.

Here's the last bit of theory for the moment. Those 12 notes? That's called the **chromatic scale**, and each note is a **semitone** (or **half-step** if you're American) apart. We don't usually use all those 12 notes in melodies. Instead, we usually use one of a number of possible combinations of around seven or eight of the notes, which have been deemed pleasing to the ear over the last few centuries.

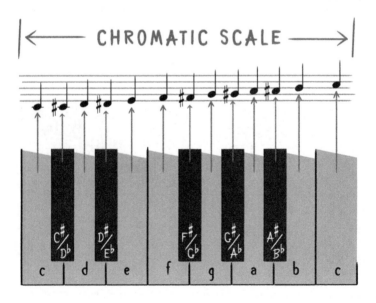

By far the most common of these are called the **major** and the **minor scale**. Most tunes and songs that you know will use one of these scales. If you jump from, say, a C3 to a C4, that's called an **octave** (eight notes).

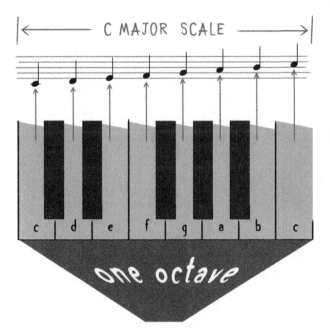

You might be familiar with 'Do Re Mi' from *The Sound Of Music*. The 'Do Re Mi Fa So La Ti Do' is the sound of the major scale, and the first and last 'Do's are an octave apart.

A quick summary of the above: there are 12 different notes, with lower and higher versions of each. We take eight of those notes and make them into a scale, and give them letter names (ABCDEFG). Some of those eight notes are closer together than others. The closer ones are deemed to be a semitone apart, while the further ones are usually a **tone** (two semitones) apart. Where there's a gap between them, the note in that gap gets named after the note on either side, so the note between D and E is either D-sharp (D#), ie, slightly higher than D, or E-flat (Eb), ie, slightly lower than E.

Watch my video about this. I use the piano keyboard to explain this a lot, as it's very well laid-out to enable you to see how it works. You'll have questions but park them for the moment, and just accept that this is how it works:

 https://lcv.pub/TYCSTA12

When you've watched and read this as much as you think you need to, move on to the next chapter, where I teach you some biology.

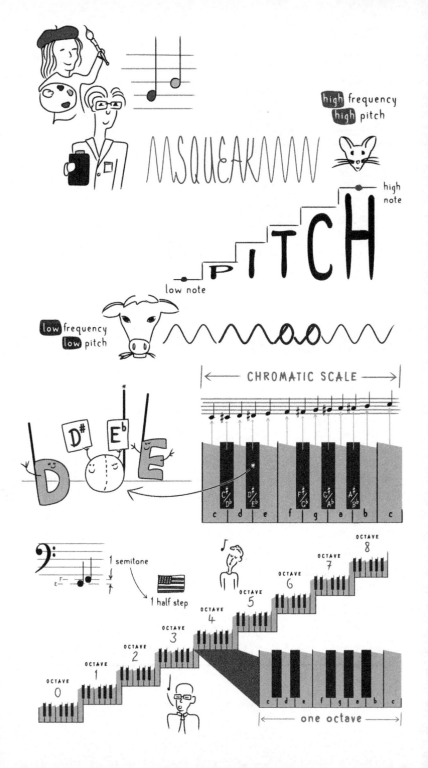

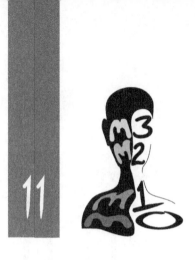

A BIT OF BIOLOGY

It's important that you have a basic understanding of the mechanism that we use to produce sound with our voices.

The **vocal folds** are flexible, complex, multi-layered structures. They're made up of at least five layers, consisting of a combination of muscle, ligament, skin and connective tissue. It's helpful to think of the vocal folds as being divided into two sections. The top two layers we can call the **cover**, and the bottom three can be referred to as the **body**.

Most of us have two distinctly different-sounding types of singing voice that we can produce. These are called **registers**. There's the strong, lower part of our voice, where most of us speak from, and there's the high part of our voice which we might use if we were to imitate a whimpering puppy or a cat miaowing. The difference tends to be more obvious in men, as they generally have lower speaking voices than women.

For years and years, the strong lower voice has been referred to as the **chest voice**, and the higher, airy voice as the **head voice**, as that is often where these sounds appear to resonate, but these are misleading terms. Head voice is also often called **falsetto** – again, a misleading term, as it is very much a real part of the voice. I'll use these definitions for the next couple of paragraphs and then I will re-educate you on how it really works. For some more examples of head voice, listen to 'Stayin' Alive' by the Bee Gees:

https://lcv.pub/TYCSTA-BG

Also have a listen to the 'Wooo' at the end of every verse of 'Twist & Shout' by the Beatles:

 https://lcv.pub/TYCSTA_T-S

So, how it actually works is this. When we use our normal voice – our speaking voice – both the body and the cover are vibrating. As you sing or speak higher in pitch, both the body and the cover stretch, but after a certain point, due to its construction, the body is unable to stretch further and no longer vibrates, leaving the cover to vibrate on its own.

To reiterate, when both **body and cover** are vibrating, this is the register that lots of people call chest voice, and when **just the cover** is vibrating, this is the higher register known as head voice or falsetto.

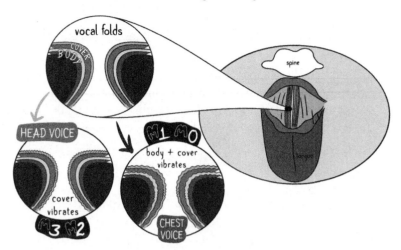

We're going to rename them **M1** (chest voice) and **M2** (head voice). M stands for mechanism (referring to the laryngeal mechanism, or simply 'how it works'). I'm going to use the definitions of M1 and M2 from now on.

There are actually two more registers as well – **M0** and **M3**.

M0 is often called **vocal fry**, and doesn't really have a specific pitch. If you were to imitate a door creaking, or a pretend burp, you'd use M0. This is when both the body and the cover are both loosely vibrating.

M3 is also referred to as **whistle** register, and is extremely high.

Listen to the chorus from Minnie Riperton's 'Loving You', after the 'doot 'n doo, do doo' the next bit is super-high, and is in M3. In M3, the vocal folds are stretched very thin and tightly:

 https://lcv.pub/TYCSTA-MR

Have a look at this video, showing the vocal folds in action. It will hopefully give you some understanding of how the mechanisms work.

 https://lcv.pub/TYCSTA-LARYNX

So, to recap:

M0 – croaky, vocal fry

M1 – normal speaking/singing voice (chest)

M2 – high singing voice (head, falsetto)

M3 – whistle

As a new singer, one of the things you need to get used to is the fact that as you go up and down your range (the distance between your lowest and highest notes), you will find that there is a break in between your M1 and M2 registers. As you become more proficient at singing, you can learn to minimise this break and smooth it over so that it's almost imperceptible. However, for the moment, be assured that it's perfectly normal, and it isn't damaging your voice. Lots of people wince when they sing across that break, as they think they're doing something bad to their voice. They're not. Yodellers make a feature of this break. So did Tarzan. Explore it, and don't be frightened of it. Think of it more as changing gear when driving. It's all part of the process.

There is an overlap between the notes covered by M1 and M2, so there are some notes that you will be capable of producing in either register. Which one you choose will depend upon a number of factors, such as the type of music you're singing, how loud you want it, the **timbre** or voice quality that you want to produce, how much breath you have available, and more.

TLDR

- We all have multiple registers or types of voice which we can learn to access.

- The two main registers are called M1 (speaking voice) and M2 (Bee Gees or puppy voice).

- The break in between these is perfectly natural and when you sing across it, it isn't hurting your voice.

- These two registers overlap, so sometimes you'll be able to select which register you assign to certain notes.

Have a look at my video about this, where I actually demonstrate what I mean by the different registers, and what they sound like:

 https://lcv.pub/TYCSTA13

Once you've watched this, move on to the next chapter, which is all about memory.

MEMORY, MUSCLE MEMORY AND WAYPOINTS

Here are some tips that should help while you're getting your head around all this new information. You need to start to engage your memory with tunes, and to do this actively. It won't just happen by osmosis. You have to make an effort to try and learn how the tune goes. 'How do I do that?' I hear you ask. Well, here are some tips...

1. Focus on the twists and the turns

We have to learn how to remember a tune before we can sing it back. It doesn't just happen passively. In the same way that just looking at a piece of paper with words on it will not allow most people to recall all those words after 30 minutes, looking at a piece of paper with music on it, or hearing a piece of music will not automatically commit that tune to memory. It has to be a 'fully present and aware' activity. Start by focusing on general things like

- Is it mostly high or low?

- Are the notes mainly long, short or a mixture?

- Do you notice any big leaps from high to low or vice versa?

Then you need to become more specific:

- Is the first note high or low?

- Is it short or long?

- What happens next?

- Does it stay on the same note?

- Does it move up or down?

- Are there any surprising things about the tune?

Going back to something I mentioned earlier, think about the way that we remember directions. Let's say that you come to my home for a weekend, which we'll assume you've never visited. I then decide to take you for a walk, but I tell you that I want you to be able to take the exact same walk the next day, but you have to lead. What would you do? You'd make notes, possibly on your phone, maybe in a notebook, possibly just in your head. 'Ok, all the way to the end, then turn right. Turn left by the church. Turn left into the park, then a right after the lake..., etc.' If you didn't take note of the twists and turns like this, you wouldn't be successful at all in reconstructing the walk the next day. Listening to music in order to sing/play it is just like this. You have to start noticing the waypoints.

2. Make sure you practise the right starting note

Often in a rehearsal, when I give starting notes to sections, I'll hear some people sing a note that I didn't give them. They sort of think that they're getting ready – 'limbering up', if you will – but actually what they're doing is increasing the likelihood that they sing the wrong notes.

If you're going to sing the starting note before you actually start the song, make sure that it's the same as the one that you've just been given. This is an example of 'that'll do' mentality, which is unhelpful, and it's borne out of lack of understanding. The person concerned thinks that it's enough to sing a note – any note – and that will prepare their voice for the next bit of singing. If it's not accurate, however, preparing like this is likely to make things worse.

3. Wait for the bigger picture

Some people, when attempting to learn a new melody, have a poor strategy. Rather than listening carefully to the whole tune a few times before attempting it, they try and sing the phrase at the same time as they listen to it. This means that they don't really ever take in the relationships between the notes, or the shape of the melody. Instead, their effort goes into trying to pitch each note immediately as it happens. It's inevitably unsuccessful, and they rarely learn how the tune actually goes.

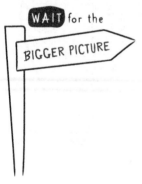

Another example. If I were to recite a poem to you, and to ask you to recite it back as accurately as you could, would it be better to (a) repeat each word in turn immediately as soon as I'd said it (a bit like you might have done at school, trying to annoy people by copying them), or (b) listen to me recite the poem first a couple of times and then try to get as much right as you could? Which would give you better recall? The answer is (b) of course, because with (a) your brain isn't actively trying to remember the sense of what is being said. You need to get the bigger picture, and be engaging your brain to notice details such as those I mentioned in the previous paragraph.

4. Judge the gap

Judging the gap can be tricky. Ask anyone who has ever tried to parallel-park. I've got a lazy left eye, and I occasionally misjudge the width of doorways. Pouring wine into a glass, I have to move my head physically to check that the bottle is in fact in the same plane as the glass, as I've been known to pour it straight onto the table.

We have this amazing thing called muscle memory, which allows us to remember what it feels like to do a certain thing. Muscle memory is a misnomer though. As I mentioned before, it's not actually stored in the muscles – it's stored in the brain. When I was 14 years old, I learned a piano transcription of 'Cavatina', the guitar music used in the film *The Deer Hunter*. I can still remember lots of it today, not because I've played it loads over the past few years (I haven't), but because my brain established those neural pathways by practising, and I can do it even while having a conversation with someone.

There are countless examples of muscle memory, one of the most obvious being driving. Our brain can allow our hands and feet to move certain distances without thinking about it. Neuropsychologists call this procedural memory, and it's stored in the basal ganglia in the brain. This is a separate part of the brain from the bit where you keep the memory of what you did at the weekend or, indeed, what you just came into this room for. There are cases where, for example, people with total amnesia can sit down and play the piano, because this muscle memory is stored somewhere different from the damaged part of the brain. Technically, the way to describe this properly is that they are exhibiting intact procedural memory while suffering from impaired declarative memory. Read up about the rather sad case of Clive Wearing:

 https://lcv.pub/TYCSTA-CW

It also happens the other way around. People with Parkinson's Disease often have intact declarative memory and impaired procedural memory, meaning that they might remember that they CAN play the piano, but then can't actually play anymore.

Singers use muscle memory a lot, on many of different levels. One of the most basic of these is judging the gap between two notes. You have to begin to feel what it's like to sing one note, then another note very close but slightly higher, or a note an octave lower. The pitch gap between two notes is called an **interval**, and each interval has a name. I could go into all the details of this now, but it's better for you to learn that stuff on a need-to-know basis.

In fact, I think that's the key to good music education. Everything should be on a need-to-know basis. Many potentially great musicians have been lost because their music teachers were trying to stuff them full of irrelevant information too early. When I teach piano to someone from scratch, I usually don't teach them music notation for quite a long time. I do, however, often teach them bits of theory normally reserved for much more advanced pupils. This is because I deem these particular bits of theory to be essential, but the notation (while extremely useful) is unnecessary at the beginning.

What you do need to know now is that different intervals feel different to sing, because they require different stretches of muscles in the throat. Notes that are close together in pitch feel completely different to sing from notes that are far apart. When you start to learn what these differences in interval feel like, those differences will be stored in your procedural memory. Right now, don't be concerned that this is all new. It's like when you're learning to dance, or do martial arts, or in fact any activity that requires you to make a body part travel a certain distance at a certain angle. You have to practise movements very deliberately for a while before they become second nature. Eventually your brain will learn how to do this movement more efficiently and more accurately, and you'll be able to do it without thinking consciously about it. But you have to actually make those neural pathways before they start becoming memories. Imagine a field that is in between an estate and a newly-built school. The field is about to become the shortcut to the school. At first it will start out even all over, the grass undisturbed. After about the first week of term, there will be some footprints, and a definite flattening of the grass along a certain path. As time goes on, that path will be worn down so that it looks like it has always been there. One day it might even get paved. This is an illustration of how the pathways will build up in the brain. At the moment, you've got a pretty grassy field there. You need to make some footprints.

TLDR

- You have to put a bit of effort into learning how the tune goes, noting the twists and turns.

- It's important to really listen to the whole melody, rather than just trying to sing each note as it happens, so that you understand the overall shape of the tune.

- It's crucial to learn to judge the gap between the notes (the interval).

Watch this video, where I break down some of these tips and tricks related to memory:

 https://lcv.pub/TYCSTA14

After you've finished, move on to the next video, where you're going to learn to make some of those 'footprints' in your neural pathways.

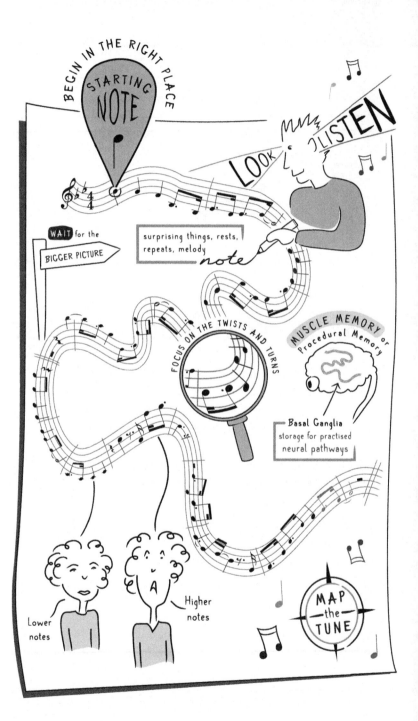

MAKING FOOTPRINTS

In order to make these footprints in your memory, which will eventually become worn grass, then a mud footpath, and then maybe even paved over at some point, we need to do some focused listening.

I've mentioned before that the pitch gap between two notes is called an **interval**. There are intervals of differing sizes; sometimes they go up and sometimes down. This is what makes melodies interesting. A variety of intervals keeps our brains stimulated. You need to become familiar with what some of the main types of interval sound like.

Semitones

We're going to start with the basic building block in Western music culture – the **semitone** (or if you're

American, half-step). I'm not (I'm Irish South-African!) so I'm going to use the term semitone.

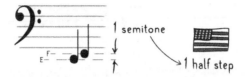

The semitone is the smallest interval (distance between pitches) in our Western music system. You can get smaller gaps (**microtones**), but we don't use them much, although other cultures do (Indian, for example), and there is increasing use of them in some experimental dance music.

Let's not get bogged down in this at the moment. So, our unit of musical currency with relation to pitch is a semitone. That's all very well knowing that, but what does it sound like, and what does it feel like to sing?

I'm going to assume you've seen the film *Jaws*. If you haven't, go and watch it immediately. Or at least watch this:

https://lcv.pub/TYCSTA-JAWS

Most people are familiar with the scene at the beginning of the film, where the woman is swimming at dusk. You hear the menacing two notes from the double bass, then a silence, then the same notes again, then again, but faster... Those two notes pretty much won John Williams an Oscar. They are a semitone apart. You should be able to hear that they're really close together in pitch.

Have a listen to the beginning of Beethoven's 'Für Elise', one of the best-known piano pieces in the world. Those repeating notes at the beginning – they're a semitone apart:

 https://lcv.pub/TYCSTA-FE

Can you hear the similarity between *Jaws* and 'Für Elise'?

Here's some more contemporary-style music, 'Cha Cha Cha', by Käärijä. Have a listen. You should be able to hear that the first minute and a half of this track are based around the semitone:

 https://lcv.pub/TYCSTA-EUROVISION

Now, I mentioned in an earlier chapter that in the musical scale there are 12 different notes, each a semitone apart, after which the scale repeats itself with higher and lower versions of itself depending on which direction you move. If we start on an A2 and move up a semitone every time, after 12 of these gaps, we'll arrive at the similar-but-different sounding A3. Do the same again 12 times and we'll end up at A4. And so on. This bigger gap between A2 and A3, for example, is an **octave**. This is another one of those intervals which you just need to be able to recognise.

Octaves

Octaves are everywhere. We use them in all sorts of situations. We already talked about the octave with reference to the third line of 'Happy Birthday'. 'Somewhere Over The Rainbow' just wouldn't be the same without those first two notes, an octave apart – 'Some - where...':

https://lcv.pub/TYCSTA-RAINBOW

Another example is Billy Joel's 'Piano Man'. At the start of each verse he's just crooning away easily – 'It's nine o'clock on a Saturday...' – and then suddenly he's there in force - 'He says, "Son, can you play me a memory?..."':

https://lcv.pub/TYCSTA-PIANOMAN

Those two sections sound sort of the same but also different. They're an octave apart. The first is easily within Billy's speaking register, so he can casually and effortlessly croon the notes. They're strong without him having to go to much effort. The second section, however, is much higher in pitch, and requires the application of some technique in order to sing the notes. You can hear the effort it takes to push those high notes out. They're not hard for him to get, as he has a great range, but he definitely has to put in more effort than with the first section.

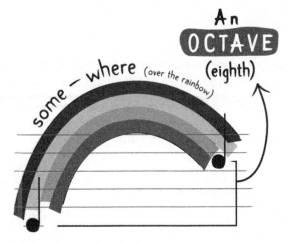

It's important to be able to identify the octave gap. Occasionally in my choir rehearsals, someone will come along who I can hear is probably a bass, the lowest of the voices. I'll start to teach the basses their part, and I'll hear someone singing the same tune but really low, the octave below where it's supposed to be. It's always tricky to explain this to the newbie, as it sounds to them like they're singing the correct note – and in a sense, they are – it's just in the wrong octave. However, when you're in a choir, it's important to be able to identify the correct octave at which to sing, because certain harmonic effects will be dependent on you doing so. It doesn't mean it's wrong to sing down there, but when the music calls for it to be at a certain octave, then it needs to be sung there. It's hard to find an analogy, but for example, imagine you are in a play. Let's suppose the directions read [said in an American accent] but you delivered the lines in a Scottish accent. You've got the right words, and out of context there's nothing wrong with saying them in a Scottish accent, but it's not appropriate for what the writer wanted.

We're going to look at one more interval for the moment.

Fifths

Fifths are everywhere, too – almost as common as octaves. Here are some examples. The main themes of these tunes either start with or are based around a fifth:

'The Last Post':

https://lcv.pub/TYCSTA-LASTPOST

Star Wars:

https://lcv.pub/TYCSTA-SW

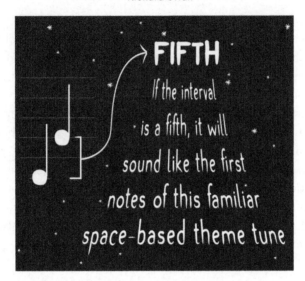

ET:

https://lcv.pub/TYCSTA-ET

Superman:

https://lcv.pub/TYCSTA-SUPERMAN

'Also sprach Zarathustra' (theme from 2001):

https://lcv.pub/TYCSTA-ALSO

As you can see, fifths are particularly common in massive orchestral music, especially in theme tunes. Fifths are very important in music for many reasons which I won't go into at this point. There's all sorts of maths involved which we just don't need to talk about now, but which I find really satisfying. Google it if you're interested.

For singing, a fifth is about halfway between a semitone (the smallest gap) and an octave (the big one we learned about in the last chapter). So, let's say you're going to sing a note, and then sing a second note that is a fifth above the first one. Once you've sounded the first note, your brain has to learn to make your throat muscles adjust so that they take the pitch higher than the semitone... keep going... keep going... and stop a fair bit before you get to the octave. How do you know how far to go? Well, as before, it's a combination of listening and muscle memory. One part of your brain recalls what it feels like to move a fifth gap, another part of your brain recalls and anticipates the note that you would expect to hear, another part again double checks that the note you are singing correlates with the expected sound. Once you get good at this, even more bits of your brain will be pressed into service, doing things like adjusting the tuning if you're a bit flat or sharp, attempting to remember words, adjust your tone, breathe, keep your heart going, etc.

There aren't any more TLDRs now – the rest of the book is hard to summarise like that.

Try the exercises in the next video. They're designed to get you used to singing semitones, octaves and fifths.

When you've finished move onto the next lesson, **Lost in the Crowd**:

https://lcv.pub/TYCSTA15

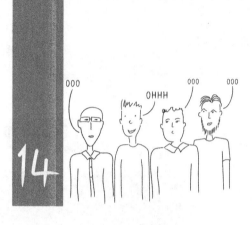

LOST IN THE CROWD

There's an old joke about the man who is on his way home late one night. As he walks past a lamppost, he sees a man on his hands and knees, rooting around in the grass under the lamp.

'What are you doing?' he asks.

'I'm looking for my keys,' says the man, pointing towards a dark bit of the pavement. 'I dropped them over there.'

'Why are you looking here, if you dropped them over there?'

'Well, the light's much better over here!'

There's something strange that happens with some people when they sing in a group. People who ordinarily can pitch perfectly well when they are singing on their own, suddenly become incapable of pitching correctly when they sing with a group, *even when everybody in the group is singing the same part as they are.* I've noticed this with my choir. People who have no problem with individually pitching notes that I sing to them start singing markedly out-of-tune when the whole section is singing in unison. Several of our members have proved in various ways that they can sing at pitch on their own, including singing quite accomplished solo songs at some of our open mic nights. However, to all intents and purposes, they seem to become tone-deaf when they sing with their section.

I've spent hours trying to work out what causes this, and it's only very recently that I've started to make sense of why it happens. For the record, I've noticed that the people in question tend to sing at a much lower pitch than they should be singing at, often three or four tones (or more) below where they need to be. Here's my theory then. I believe that the problem stems from a misguided belief among those people as to what the sensation in their throat should feel like, and they are prioritising this over the far more important task of listening to the note that they are actually producing and matching with the target note (hence the joke with which I started this chapter). There's a kind of denial going on. They think it can't be them singing out of tune as it 'feels right'.

I surmise that the mental process is going something like this:

'I know the bass part is starting soon. Right, here we go. I'm sure that it should feel about *here* in my throat, as this is where I'm strongest and it feels good. I can hear that there's someone singing the wrong notes, but it can't be me, as it feels right to be singing like this.'

As mentioned in a previous chapter (**Just the Basic Facts**), some people have also normalised the dissonance. They have desensitised themselves from the unpleasantness of the clashing notes, and simply made it ok in their heads for those notes to be wrong. If this is the case, they are much less likely to feel the need to correct the note that they are singing.

It's surprising how many people fall into this trap. I've actually fallen into it myself, when the other music that was going on was so loud that I couldn't hear myself. I estimated the pitch according to my muscle memory of the sensation, and I got it wrong.

You occasionally hear this happen at gigs and concerts, when the monitoring (ie, the mix that the performers are hearing) is mixed badly, so the singer cannot hear themselves over the backing music. A classic example of this is the Eurovision Song Contest, where they have lots of acts to set up in a short space of time, and so sometimes the sound isn't perfect for the performers. The result is usually that the singer is out-of-tune. Not, perhaps, as much as an untrained person might be, but they're still estimating what note they're singing based on the feeling in the throat, and that's often not very accurate. With a trained singer, it can sometimes be a bit sharp, as trained singers tend to understand that it's so easy to go flat, so they overcompensate.

In 2019, Madonna performed her huge hit 'Like A Prayer' at Eurovision during the interval. Something was obviously very wrong with her monitoring and she either couldn't hear herself or her backing track properly, and the result was this:

https://lcv.pub/TYCSTA-MADONNA

The conclusion we can draw from this is that it's a multi-layered issue. The combination of someone (a) not being able to hear themselves clearly enough, and (b) relying too much on what they think it should feel like to sing the correct notes can result in them pitching incorrectly.

So how do you know if you're doing this? Well, the first thing you can do is to put your finger in one of your ears (not both!) while you're singing, and try to listen to (a) your own voice, and (b) the people around you. Then you need to compare the two. Putting your finger in one ear and shifting your attention to that ear makes it easier to focus on your own voice and then quickly shift your attention to the other ear where you should be able to hear the sounds going on around you. If you discover that actually you're the one at fault, you'll have to try and correct yourself. You might find you need to stop singing and then start again, as it can be hard to shift to the new pitch while you're actually performing.

If you find that you have indeed been singing the wrong pitch when in groups, then you'll need to make a habit out of this corrective process, and go through it every single time you sing in groups, until you're confident that you're singing the correct notes automatically. You'll probably get to the stage quite soon when you don't need to put a finger in your ear, but what you will have to work quite hard at is not trusting the 'feel' of the note.

One key metric that you can use to work out whether you're doing this right is as follows. **If you're not finding some of the notes a bit hard to sing, you're probably singing some wrong notes.** You should need to put some effort in to reach some of the notes. They shouldn't all be easy to sing. You should be being exercised while you're singing. Think of it as being a bit like when you're at the gym. If it's all nice and easy, then you're doing it wrong.

Watch my video on this to understand more about this process, and to try some exercises that will make you work a bit hard. Once you've done that, move on to the next chapter, **Success Stories**, to hear about some of the people who have gone before you in this learning adventure:

https://lcv.pub/TYCSTA16

SUCCESS STORIES

You need to know that this stuff works. I can assure you that in the vast majority of cases, if you take the time to implement the tips and tricks you learn here, they will have an impact on the quality of sound that you make. Here are some case studies which you might find interesting.

By the way, I'm aware that most of these success stories are about men. The reality is that it is often boys who are discouraged from singing, either by their peers teasing them for not being manly enough, or because when their voices change at puberty, they have no one to help them navigate this brand new voice they have suddenly acquired.

John

John came to me after seeing my choir perform at an event he was attending. He seemed very nervous, but he had plucked up the courage to talk to me and say how much he'd like to be part of something like that. I invited him along to our rehearsals, emphasising that there was no audition, and that he'd be very welcome.

He came along to our rehearsal the following Tuesday, and it was immediately evident that his pitching needed some work. I could hear that the notes he was singing were nowhere near the ones I needed him to sing. I asked him to hang about a bit after the rehearsal so that I could go through a few things with him, and he was happy to do so. When I asked him to 'Sing this note', he immediately did what I mentioned earlier. He sang a random note before I'd even finished singing the reference note to him. I asked him to wait, and really listen to the note before trying to reproduce it. This time he got it straight away. We carried on with this for about 20 minutes, and then we called it a day. I asked him if he'd be ok to do the same for the next few sessions that he attended, and he agreed to do so. We had three post-rehearsal sessions, each lasting about 20 minutes. The upshot was that he improved vastly – not all the time in the beginning, but once he'd realised that you have to consciously aim for the notes, the difference became significant. He's now a strong and reliable member of the choir, and even performed a solo and as part of a duet at a couple of our choir open mic sessions.

Here's his performance of 'Love Is All Around' at an open mic. Remember, this is his first EVER solo performance. I think he nailed this:

     https://lcv.pub/TYCSTA-JMCD

Graeme

Graeme joined my choir quite early on, and was always a bit of a wild card with pitching at first. He has a rich bass voice, but in his enthusiasm at the beginning he would often make stabs in the dark with his pitching. He often didn't pitch it high enough. The reason for this was that he was underestimating the amount of effort he needed to make in order to correctly pitch the note. I spent a fair bit of time gently correcting these missed notes.

Several years on, Graeme is a reliable member of the bass section. He sang a solo – Schubert's 'Ave Maria' – at his brother's wedding, and I have accompanied him a few times singing solos at open mic nights.

Walter

I have a phrase that I use when we have people who attend our rehearsals who are struggling with pitching, and who are noticeably singing the wrong notes. It's an attempt to encourage them to listen more attentively and be Honest Self-Critics, without drawing attention to who they are. I tend to say, 'There's someone in the <insert voice part> section who isn't listening hard enough to the notes that they need to match. If that's you, just aim a bit better.' When Walter joined us, he was one of these people for several months. Then, one Wednesday evening, I was standing with the tenors in the pub during a post-rehearsal sing, and I could hear someone singing the tenor part super-accurately and powerfully. I looked up to see who it was, and it was Walter. I was gobsmacked. I asked him, 'What happened to you? When did you get so accurate?!' He said that he just made the decision to take the risk, and work hard on the parts and sing them out strongly.

That decision has really paid off. I'm very proud of him, and I'd say that he's in line to be one of our strongest tenors.

Nicola

Nicola's husband is a singer in my son Ben's choir (yes, choir-directing is hereditary). He bought his wife some lessons with me for her birthday, as she had always said she couldn't sing. She has Grade VIII piano, but would always sing out-of-tune.

She came to me rather nervous about what was going to happen, but she very quickly relaxed and started to view the experience as a lesson, rather than an ordeal. Her main issues were the usual ones: (a) not taking enough time to find the correct starting note, and (b) trying to stick to the strong parts of her voice all the time. Within two lessons, we managed to achieve a huge amount, with her understanding more and more about how her voice worked, and how she had to put more care and attention into finding the correct note to start on. Here's a recording of her singing a song from *Les Miserables*:

 https://lcv.pub/TYCSTA-NICOLA

Julio

Julio joined us in 2023. He sat in the basses, and rarely sang the right notes. He tended to drone in a monotone. One evening after a rehearsal, I demonstrated the essence of tuning, asking someone else to hold a note, while I sang just underneath the pitch, and then rising slowly until I hit the correct note (as in the video near the beginning of this book: **https://lcv.pub/TYCSTA02**). He visibly reacted when I hit the note, and suddenly appeared to understand.

A couple of weeks later, someone else was teaching a particular song in the rehearsal, and I sat next to Julio at the back of the bass section. To my amazement, he was note perfect. He said that since that demonstration, it had made sense to him, and he had been practising all weekend. He is now a regular member of the bass section, and has signed up to do an open mic session.

Rob

Rob is the husband of Lolly, one of my choir members. They both came on our singing holiday to Greece this year, but Rob just came for the fun, not the singing. He was adamant that he wasn't going to take part in any rehearsals, but I'm very persuasive and chatted about it with him on the first night. Despite having been told for more than 50 years that he couldn't sing, he agreed to come to the first rehearsal and see how it went. He was nervous, but he was true to his word and turned up and sat in the bass section. My son Ben helped him through the rehearsal, and although he wasn't very accurate at the beginning, it was clear that with a bit of work, he'd be able to do this. I sent him the manuscript of this book (unfinished at the time) for some holiday reading, and a link to the videos, and he set about improving.

This is the only thing you need to watch in order to understand what a difference this made to him. He performed this four days later, at our open mic session:

https://lcv.pub/TYCSTA-ROB

Jonny

I have a little bit more to say about Jonny, as I found him such an interesting case. Jonny joined my choir a while back with some friends. None of them had any experience in singing. Jonny has excellent timing, but from the beginning his pitching was way off, and he would sometimes sing quite loudly as well, which could be a bit off-putting to other members of the choir.

I offered him some free sessions in order to deal with this situation. At first I had some misgivings, as I wondered if he actually had amusia and would just be disappointed by my efforts. However, within about 15 minutes of him arriving at my house, I had established that without a shadow of a doubt, he did not have amusia. However, there were some definite issues with maintaining accuracy of pitch. His voice was naturally low, and he wasn't accustomed at all to using the upper range of his voice, so he tended not to use it. When I sang a low note (between his lowest note of F2 and about G3), he was fairly accurate at singing it back. If I went higher than that, it was more hit-and-miss. I believe that what was happening was that when the notes got higher, they didn't feel as right or as easy to sing, so he defaulted to a feeling in his throat which felt stronger and more comfortable, despite it not being the correct pitch. He wasn't clued-up enough on how much his pitch was off, and didn't really even consider that as an issue. Because of lots of the reasons we've already discussed in this book, he simply hadn't realised how much more effort he needed to put into aiming and checking his pitch.

Once we'd established some tricks for this – for example, the swooping up to a note worked really well – we set about performing a song. I chose to do a very slow version of 'A Little Respect', and to do it in a much lower key than it would normally be sung, due to Jonny's low range.

It took a little while, and several tries, but eventually he managed to perform the whole verse fairly accurately, with the odd note that was a bit out of place. Interestingly, a lot of the time he would sing a whole section in tune, and then be upended by one note or another, and from that point be thrown off-kilter. As I mentioned in the section on Bad Karaoke, if you start on the wrong note and then sing the tune perfectly in relation to that starting note, it's not going to sound very nice.

We also played around with vocal registers. It turned out that Jonny was often more accurate in his higher M2 register than in his M1 voice.

A couple of months later, Jonny came back to me for another lesson. In the intervening time, he had continued to attend choir rehearsals. This time he had definitely improved. We started with me singing an 'aa' over four beats with a piano accompaniment, starting on a Bb3, which he would then sing back to me. We moved up a semitone at a time, each time with me demonstrating first. He was completely successful in this all the way up to B4, which is near the top of his (M1 or chest voice) range. Once we got there, he started to lose accuracy, mainly, I think, because he didn't know how to push his M1 register any higher, and couldn't quite work out how to flip it into M2. I then skipped some notes and went higher, easily in his M2 register and way beyond his M1 range. He was immediately able to pitch the notes. We pushed this as high as we could go (about A5), and then started to descend, one semitone at a time, towards his M1 range and beyond.

What this was doing was simply giving him a chance to practise producing notes in a controlled environment, with me watching over him and giving him feedback. This enabled him to begin to learn what was right and what wasn't. If no one ever tells you that you're doing it wrong then you don't know. Or if they tell you you're doing it wrong in an unkind way, and don't give you feedback on how you can actually correct it and do it right, you'll never improve.

After about 15 minutes of just hitting notes – essentially copying me singing them – his accuracy began to get better and better. We were then able to look at the **transition range** – the set of notes served by both M1 and M2 – and begin to get used to hearing the note, then making the choice of whether to sing that note in M1 or M2.

After we'd spent another ten minutes on this, we decided to have a look at an actual song. I had suggested that Snow Patrol's 'Run' might be a good choice, as it doesn't have a huge range and it's also quite slow (giving him time to find the pitch of the notes).

We tried this in the original key, but he was really struggling with getting the high notes, and when he did manage to get them, he didn't have much breath to sing with. We then tried it really low, which worked much better for him, so we pursued this for a while. At the moment, he's practising it in this much lower key.

We then moved onto a choir song that we do, a version of 'Sit Down' by James. He got the beginning of this reasonably well, but then when the lyrics go 'Drawn by the undertow my life is out of control', in our version there's a drop to a particular note which is repeated. He kept overshooting on this bit and singing much lower than he was meant to. It was at this point that the penny dropped for me, and led me to the realisation of what I talk about in the previous chapter, **Lost in the Crowd**. He was dropping down to a note which **felt good to sing**, rather than the actual note which was situated a bit higher than he was comfortable with. Once I'd identified this as being the culprit, it was easy to explain that he needed to keep it in the 'slightly higher than you want it to be' range, and he was more accurate.

Since I started this chapter, Jonny has performed a song at one of our choir open mic nights. He sang 'Run'. It went really well, and you can hear his performance at the following link:

   https://lcv.pub/TYCSTA-JONNY

Onwards, to the last chapter. We're not done yet. There's a little more to say...

16

listen
carefully

WRAPPING IT UP

Right, so you've made it to the last chapter.
Congratulations. I really hope you've found it useful, and
that it's given you some confidence. There are a few
more things to say. Firstly, this doesn't necessarily all
happen immediately. Like with any new skill, you'll have
days when it seems easy and natural, and other days
when nothing seems to work at all. Don't be put off by
the latter. It's part of the learning curve. You will get
better at this. Stick to the facts. Remember, if you can
easily recognise tunes, you probably don't have amusia.
If you don't have amusia, you can probably learn to sing.
Those are facts. Sometimes you need to lean on those
to get through. Take your time. Practise. As I said earlier,
these are complicated procedures that the brain has to
go through, and... well... you're not as young as you used
to be! Joking aside, it's going to be harder to learn this as

an adult than as a child, as children are wired to absorb new information like a sponge. Trust my process. It does work for most people.

Here's a final task for you:

https://lcv.pub/TYCSTA17

Then have a look at my final video of this series:

https://lcv.pub/TYCSTA18

If you'd like to know more, please get in touch. Keep an eye on the website, **www.tycsta.com**, for events around this subject that might be of interest. If you'd like workshops or a talk at your conference or event, let me know.

If you feel you've made some progress, and you'd like to have some individual sessions with me, please get in touch. I'm not cheap, but it's possible to arrange, either in person or on Zoom. If you take me up on this, it will take you to the next level of development with your voice. Individual coaching sessions give you that one-to-one feedback that you simply can't get without the direct intervention of a human being.

I would say, however, at the risk of doing myself out of more business here, that the very best way of getting better at this is to go and sing in a non-audition choir, or take yourself to a (good, sympathetic) singing teacher. If you do the former, what you'll find is that there's a total mix of abilities – people who are amazing singers, people who are average, people who are the same level as you, people who are worse than you (yep, really!). And that's ok. As you sing more and more, you'll get more confident, and you'll improve at the whole thing. No, don't protest. I'm right. If you think about it, it's the same with anything. As you practise more at something, you'll get better at doing it. Practising doesn't work differently for you than for anyone else.

People who spend time regularly in London, come and get involved in our very inclusive singing family, **London City Voices**:

https://lcv.pub/TYCSTALCV

I'M GOING TO JOIN

*Other choirs are available

TO PUT IN LOTS OF PRACTICE

If you'd really like to join LCV, but you're nowhere near London, we do have an online branch of our choir, which is more than just a Zoom choir. There's actual simultaneous singing. At the time of writing, we have members regularly joining us from Canada, the USA and Germany. Check out the above link and follow the links through to the online rehearsals.

One of the fantastic things that came out of the COVID pandemic is the fact that lots of choir directors bonded online across the world, so there are some fantastic networks who will be happy to help you find a singing family near to you. One such network in the UK (but with international members too) is MD Brunch, who will be very happy to help you to look for a choir that might suit you.

Be prepared to shop around for a choir. There are all sorts of choirs, and because they're made up of human beings, they all have their idiosyncrasies. There are some amazing ones out there, but there are also some that aren't so welcoming, especially to people who aren't very experienced at singing. Find one that is. If you're struggling to find one, get in touch with MD Brunch:

https://lcv.pub/TYCSTA-MDB

Here's a little tip to keep in mind which should help you to be more accurate with your singing. Remember way back in the beginning of the book when I talked about people launching in to try and sing the note before they actually listened to it properly? Take note of this. Before you try to sing the note, try to ascertain whether it's going to be high, medium or low in your voice. If you're the same gender as the person singing the note that you're trying to copy, try to get your voice ready. For example, if you're a man, and it's a man singing, then if it sounds like they're singing a high note, prepare yourself to put in a bit of work to sing a high note. If you're a woman, and you can hear that it's a man singing, if they're singing a high note, that's probably going to translate as quite a low note for you. You'll get the hang of this the more you do it.

Other things to keep in mind

In the early stages at least, you need to be **fully present, deliberate and aware** of what you're doing at all times when you sing. You can't afford to let the concentration lapse yet. Remember that while others may be able to hit the notes effortlessly, you must assume that for the moment, you have to focus hard in order to be accurate.

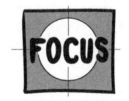

You have to be conscious of which notes you're aiming for, and work hard at getting them exactly right, and then constantly referring back to make sure that you're still getting it right. Eventually this will become second nature, but it won't start out like that.

Keep in mind the other factors that you have to pay attention to: backing music, speed, starting note, as well as other people who might be playing or singing.

Try to step back from yourself and analyse what's going on when you're singing. Are you actually singing the note you're supposed to? How about there? And there? You'll come to realise that this is a process that you have to go through for every single note. Every. Single. Note. It'll get to be automatic soon enough, but in order for that to happen, it needs to be practised over and over again. Even if you're someone who picks things up quickly, you're probably going to have to do a fair bit of work to get those footprints turning into pathways in your brain.

I could go on and on, but like I said in my final video, I'd just be rambling. Please keep an eye on the website **www.tycsta.com** for the latest links, join the online support community if you can, and KEEP AT IT!

Thank you for reading the book, and I hope this launches you into a new life with singing as a part of it. All the best.

Richard Swan
September 2023

HAVING READ AND UNDERSTOOD THIS BOOK,
I BELIEVE RICHARD SWAN IS RIGHT
AND THAT I,

_____

CAN SING!

FROM NOW ON,
I WILL COMMIT TO MAKING SURE THAT I

FOCUS · listen carefully · KEEP IN TIME · aim · will be an honest self-critic

I'M GOING TO JOIN

London* City Voices

TO PUT IN LOTS OF PRACTICE

and sing happily ever after

*Other choirs are available

Approximately 2.5% of the population are born with **congenital amusia** – the scientific name for tone-deafness. This means that they are the musical equivalent of colourblind. There's something slightly misfiring in their brain which results in them having a lower degree of musical perception than the rest of the population. If you'd like to find out if you have amusia, then you can go to this website and take a short study (it should take about 15 minutes) to find out where you stand:

https://lcv.pub/TYCSTA-BRAMS

Now, congenital amusia is on a sliding scale, rather than being a thing that you either have or haven't got, but if you find that you do have amusia, I'm afraid that I'm not going to be able to help you very much. You might find that you improve in a few ways through some of the exercises, and some of your perception may develop a little, but as Tim Falconer says in his book, *Bad Singer: The Surprising Science of Tone-Deafness And How We*

Hear Music, '...I have a bad connection in my head. And unfortunately, I can't just hang up and dial again.'

It's definitely worth giving his book a read. It's well written and very informative, and goes into lots of detail on the science of the brain and music. I haven't done that very much here, as this is a how-to book. If it turns out that you do have amusia but you'd still like to sing, there may be some groups where you can do this and not worry about what you sound like. In the UK we have the Tuneless Choir (**https://lcv.pub/TYCSTA-TUNELESS**) where they don't mind how out-of-tune you might be.

HOWEVER, the likelihood is that you don't have congenital amusia. I have written this book very specifically for those of you – about 14.5% of the population – who believe or have been told by others that you can't sing, but who **do not** have congenital amusia. Take the test at the beginning of this chapter and see how you score. If you do reasonably well on that, then it is very likely that this book will help you. For the rest of this book, unless otherwise specified, you can assume that when I've talked about people who think they can't sing, I was referring to those who have wrongly diagnosed themselves (or been told by someone else) that they are tone-deaf, but who do not have amusia. That will be most of you, to be honest. I'll say it again, **you probably don't have congenital amusia**.

Printed in Great Britain
by Amazon